WHEN GOOD BOOBS GO BAD; Cut Them Out of Your Life!

Lisa Woods

Cover design/original painting by Sonya Dilley,
SonnyD Artistry (www.facebook.com/SonnyDArtistry)

ISBN: 979-8-4844-1228-0

FOR MY MOM,
THE MOST AMAZING WOMAN I KNOW!

Thank you for your love, support, and for being the ultimate example of strength and endurance. You show me that I can survive anything life throws my way. I am who I am because you are who you are. Thank you for being there to guide my way, wipe my tears, my nose, and my butt. I appreciate your sacrifices and am honored to be the one person who can call you Mom!
I love you more than I can fully express!

FOR MY BOYS.
Thank you for being my biggest cheerleaders, for indulging my crazy and for making my life whole.
Momma loves you big!

FOR MY DAD,
Thank you for encouraging my love of writing and desire to publish a book.
I finally did it! I know you would have been proud.

WHEN GOOD BOOBS GO BAD; Cut Them Out of Your Life!

PINK PROLOGUE

Once upon a time, my life was cruising along at a moderate speed, then breast cancer punched me square in the chest. Having a strong family history of the disease, it wasn't a surprise, but it wasn't exactly on my bucket list, either.

From the moment I received the ominous phone call about a question on my routine mammogram, life as I knew it shifted course. A roadblock was placed in my path and the direction I had been heading was no longer an option. I was rerouted toward strange territory where detours would be many, and absolutes would be few. It was as if being guided by a GPS that keeps recalculating to the point that you have no idea which way you should be going, so you randomly choose a turn and end up somewhere you don't think you should be. You wind up in a place where nothing looks familiar, the signs don't make sense and all you can do is be sure your doors are locked and speed ahead hoping you have enough gas to get out of there and back to the road that you started on. It was like entering a new dimension where nothing would ever be as it once was. I was left to navigate, sometimes in the dark, and find my way in a new reality.

I have always enjoyed writing; it's one of the best ways I know to express myself. After diagnosis and once a treatment plan was in place, I felt that I needed to document my impending journey. I started a Facebook blog entitled, *When Good Boobs Go Bad, Lisa's Odyssey*. That seemed like a good way to free myself from what was going on while also informing my family and friends.

As I was not extremely social media savvy, I opened the page as public not knowing what that could lead to. It literally made a world of difference. I gained connections all over the country and at various points around the globe. Contact through the page by family, friends, friends of friends, and strangers who had been or were in the middle of the fight or just wanted to provide support and encouragement showed me that the decision to write about it and put it all out there, was a good one. I am extremely grateful for the relationships that were nurtured through that blog.

This book is an extension of that. Here you will find diary posts from the blog showing what was happening and what I was feeling at the time. Additional writing among the entries is there to expand on, explain, support, or provide anecdotes that I didn't put out in the social media world. I am not a doctor, nor do I play one on TV. These pages contain my thoughts and opinions and some things that may have worked for me, but do not supersede official medical advice or treatment plans set forth by a doctor.

Here it is, a raw and honest look into the life of a breast cancer warrior whose world has been painted pink. These pages are filled with laughter and tears; pain and encouragement; trials and triumphs along with a healthy dose of humor. The events depicted are real and names have not been changed to protect the innocent.

PART
I

In the Beginning...

SOMETHING MALIGNANT THIS WAY COMES

On July 9, 2014, I was diagnosed with breast cancer. I was 44 years old, mother to two teenage boys and a second-time newlywed, married just nine months earlier. I had no plans at that time to add cancer fighter to my list of personal descriptors but, as they say, "the best-laid plans..." These writings chronicle my physical and emotional journey in a quest to eliminate cancer and move on with my life. The goal is to encourage women (and men, too) to be vigilant about their breast health.

July 13, 2014

Initial entry in my Facebook blog, *When Good Boobs Go Bad, Lisa's Odyssey*

It finally happened, one of my boobs has gone rogue and is trying to kill me. WTH! Why has it turned on me? What did I ever do to it? The worst part is, it's the "good" boob. It's the bigger and more nicely shaped of the two, the one my husband pays a little more attention to. Why has it forsaken me? In all fairness, I

3

guess it isn't a deliberate act of attempted homicide, but rather an organic action that couldn't be stopped. I am blessed to have a huge, crazy, loving, wonderful family, the problem is, the women on my mom's side seem to be born with a giant bullseye on their chest.

My grandma's sister was the first that I know of, to be struck by breast cancer. She died either before I was born or when I was very young. I just found out about her and don't know much about the situation. She was followed by my aunt, then my mom, then my mom again, then my grandma, then another aunt, then, last year, the last of my mom's (then) living sisters and, just recently, the first aunt again. Six women, eight occurrences, three survivors, and three victims. My fate was written long ago. It was not so much a matter of IF I would be diagnosed, but when. I had gone faithfully every year for about nineteen years for a mammogram and then held my breath waiting to get the letter saying that it was all good. I knew one day I wouldn't get the letter; I would get a phone call. This year I got that call.

That's when things got real!

I was number seven of the women in my family to be handed a breast cancer diagnosis. As of this writing, number eight has taken her title. It's an unfortunate family legacy. With so much of it in my surroundings, it was always a thought in the back of my mind. After my mom's second diagnosis, I began having yearly mammograms. I had just given birth to my first son. I was 26.

I had no qualms each year as I happily allowed a mammogram tech to tape little metal BBs to my nipples and then squash my breasts into pancakes. The BBs give a point of reference for the films. More than once, I forgot to take them off and was surprised upon undressing. One time, I even had a real WTF moment when I made it into the shower with one still on.

Those mammograms were always followed by the all-important doctor letter stating that the radiology report showed nothing abnormal, until that one time that it didn't. The dreaded phone call that I had always expected came instead.

July 13, 2014

When I went to lunch the Monday after my mammogram on that previous Friday, I had two messages on my phone. One from my doctor's office and one from the radiologist. Crap! That wasn't good! I called back and was told that they saw something in the recent pictures that looked different than last year. The

5

nurse tried to reassure me that it could be a shadow on the film or bad positioning during the mammogram. I knew better but tried to convince myself that just might be it. I needed that to get me through until another mammogram a few days later.

I went into the clinic first thing Thursday morning, July 3. We were granted a rare jeans day at work to celebrate the 4th, so there I was, comfortable in my jeans, wearing an American flag scarf, looking festive, feeling sick. I got called back and was greeted by a kind woman who gently directed me into the mammogram room. This time it would target one spot. She was going to need to go in a little tight. As this gentle woman pressed my breast into the plastic vise, she apologized for what she was about to do and told me to let her know when I couldn't take it anymore. She lowered the top plate down farther and farther and then began to manually crank it tighter. If you haven't had a mammogram, you may not have a good picture of this, but let's say that you would be amazed at just how flat you can smash a breast. It is an odd situation, to say the least. I will always advocate for mammograms, though. The discomfort is minor and very brief. A couple of pictures later, it was done, and I was heading down for an ultrasound.

I laid there during the ultrasound watching the screen. I saw it. There it was a dark circular area with solid color and irregular border. The tech was marking it to measure it. I hated that it was there! Next, she softly told me that she was just going to look under my arm. I knew she was looking at lymph nodes. It was done and off she went to talk to the radiologist. Technology has made everything so much faster. It was only a couple of minutes before the radiologist was sitting in front of me telling me that there was something there and it needed to be biopsied. I expected it and I knew what I saw wasn't good, but it still took the wind out of me like a punch in the gut. It took a couple of minutes to clear my tears and get it together and then I was off for a biopsy.

I was given the opportunity to go directly from the ultrasound for the biopsy. I was told that if I went over then, they would squeeze me in. Yes, please! I had already been squeezed once that day, why not! I knew, though, that meant some waiting. I arrived at the next location a little shaky with my chest pounding. Mammography had called over and they were expecting me, so when I checked in, it was known why I was there. The older lady at the desk was barely audible when she whispered and asked if I was there for the "breast biopsy". I guess it was supposed to be a secret. I took a seat where I could see a TV screen or look out the window; options for distraction that didn't help. It's so hard to turn your mind off when you have nothing but time to sit there and think. It was starting to sink in, and I didn't really like where it was going.

About an hour later I found myself lying there looking at that spot on the screen again while a radiologist stuck a needle into my left breast and snatched out three tissue samples. When she was done, she asked if I had a surgeon in mind. Well, NO! I told her that I didn't want a surgeon, I wanted her to call and tell me that it was nothing and there was nothing to do about it. She gently told me that she would love to do that, but we had to be realistic with my family history. She could tell that it was solid and not a cyst. For the second time that day, I cried in front of strangers. It's okay, they were the same strangers that I had shown my breasts to. By the end of my appointments that day, I had shown my boobs to four strangers. Not a typical day; it's never usually more than three. Those who aren't close to me, please know that I'm joking. It's never actually been more than two. It was done, time to wait.

The radiologist who did the biopsies was also named Lisa. I took that as a good omen. She was a cancer survivor herself and told me that as a means of comfort. It helped. Her husband would end up being the surgeon to perform my mastectomy.

Time moved at a snail's pace between the biopsy and actual diagnosis. It was just six days from one to the other, but it could have been a year. When faced with the weight of a life-changing possibility, you can do everything imaginable to distract yourself, but the mind doesn't always get the message and can just keep circling back. Having cancer was on my mind all the time. I cried in the quiet moments when I was alone and worried about everything the rest of the time. I fretted over the thought of surgery. I had only ever been in the hospital to have my children and both times were rather routine. The only type of surgery that I had had was the removal of my wisdom teeth. That was quick, mostly painless and the body parts that I left behind in the office, were unimportant and unnecessary. I didn't know what to expect, or what pain would come from it.

I feared leaving my boys and wondered what would happen with them if I wasn't around. Although they were both teens at that point, they weren't ready to navigate life fully on their own and still needed my guidance. The hardest part was being quiet about it around them. I didn't want to say anything and worry them until I knew for sure (in my heart, I knew, but still needed the official call). My husband and I whispered and talked in code when they were within earshot.

One of the sillier areas of worry was having things around the house cleaned out in anticipation of someone else going through them. To my chagrin, I'm a perpetually disorganized procrastinator. That translates into having a lot of stuff that would be unfortunate for a loved one to have to sort and disperse. There are things that need to be thrown out, things that need to be organized, things that just don't belong, and odds and ends shoved in nooks and crannies in a house that I had been in for nearly 20 years by that time. There would be much for my family to go through and decide what to do with if I should suddenly be removed involuntarily from the picture.

That is part of what was swirling around in my head those six everlasting days before diagnosis. Those worries were amplified once it was official. I aspire to live by the notion that worrying about things that haven't happened or that cannot be changed is fruitless, but it's hard to shove those concerns out of your brain.

S#!T GETS REAL

July 16, 2014

It has been a week since I received my diagnosis. The doctor called around 8:00 am, July 9, 2014. She said the results of the biopsy showed cancer. My response was, "I knew that." With a slight laugh, she said she had just told that to her nurse who was concerned about her calling me at work. Doc felt sure that I already knew and that I would want confirmation as soon as possible. She and I had many conversations through the years about the plan of action if this should arise. I did expect the diagnosis, but it still struck me like a slap in the face. I feel sorry for the coworker who was in my office at the time. It's an awkward spot to be in.

It took me a few minutes to get over the initial shock and then my new reality took hold. At noon, I was sitting in the waiting room of the surgeon's office next to my sweet husband who was a little quieter than usual. Those of you who know him, know that means he was all but silent. I sat there babbling about everything that I had discussed with my doctor and what I thought the next step was and anything I could think of to try and take away from where we were. He just looked at me lovingly, held my hand, rubbed my leg, and kissed my forehead. I am so thankful that he is on this journey with me to hold my hand and kiss my forehead. The love in his eyes gives me so much strength! I can't even imagine going through this when I was on my own or even years before. It would have been so different.

The details are this: the tumor is small, about half an inch in diameter; it is stage 1; the lymph nodes looked good in ultrasound, and they don't appear to be involved. The surgeon explained that I have Invasive Ductal Carcinoma, "your everyday, garden variety breast cancer", the most common type. That is a relief, of sorts, because that means they see it all the time and know what to do with it. If ever I didn't want to be a special case, this is the time. I was the fourth patient with this by noon that day. After explaining what it is, the surgeon proceeded to talk about how we deal with it. It could be removed with an outpatient lumpectomy followed by a few weeks of radiation. That would be the typical course of action in most cases like this. In my case, that wouldn't be the best choice.

With the history in my family, I would be back doing it again at some point. Five years, ten years, 20 years down the road, it would strike again. I would always be waiting and hoping that they would find it soon enough. I don't want that forever hanging over my head. I have thought for years about what I would do if this day arrived. I had said that the first time something was found in my mammogram I would get rid of all of it. Take my boobs and give me ones that won't kill me. That day had come; time to put up or shut up.

I told the doctor that I knew the lumpectomy wasn't for me and that I needed to eliminate the possibility of this in the future. He said that is what he was going to tell me. In reviewing my personal medical history, he noted that being young and "in perfect health", I was a great candidate for surgery. I agreed that I was in good health "except for this cancer that I have". Yes, I'm that much of a smart ass. I was trying to keep it light. Not sure Dr. W. knew what to think of me. I thought very highly of him, though, and trust that he is the man for the job and will take care of this. I will be having a complete double mastectomy with reconstruction. Next stop was the plastic surgeon to talk about the changing landscape of my chest.

The radiologist who performed the biopsies led me in the direction of a surgeon, her husband. That surgeon happened to be the one who saved my Uncle Bill's life many years earlier after a horrific motorcycle accident that could have been his end. Dr. W. was a new, young surgeon at the time who my mom credits with her brother still being with us to this day. I'm a firm believer in everything happening for a reason. It was as if all was pre-determined and falling into place.

July 18, 2014

Here's the post where it gets candid. Recovery from mastectomy surgery, I was told, wouldn't be too long or involved, if it was just that surgery. Adding in reconstruction is what makes it more difficult, more painful, and a longer, more involved situation. It takes months to be complete. I had been researching all of this from the time I got the phone call about my original mammogram. I had looked at "after" pictures where there had been no reconstruction; I know I'm not strong enough to do that. I have great respect for the women who can and who wear the badge of survival on their chests without implants or rebuilt breasts: that's just not me. My breasts do not define me, but I have become accustomed to them being there.

I wasn't even blessed with boobs until after I had my kids. My cups haven't run over by any means but going from an A to a B was huge! I like having just a bit there to fill out my shirt and I admit to having played up my cleavage on occasion. I have become attached to my chest. Honestly, the thought of having my girls cut off, analyzed, and sent off as medical scrap is a little disheartening. A lot, really!

There was a discussion earlier this week with someone dear to my heart, and with the same twisted sense of humor, about keeping a couple of souvenirs, namely my nips. It went from keeping them in a jar to a key chain or necklace, giving them to Eric, etc. I'm sorry if that is unsettling to any of you, but the more we went on, the harder we laughed. You gotta laugh! They will be removed, but I'm sure they won't let me keep them. Will I ask? Maybe. When my son had his appendix out at the age of 11, I asked if we could have it. He was horrified that I would inquire on such a thing. I remember my grandma having her kidney stones in a bottle, so it wasn't that out there to request. The answer, of course, was "no", but the doctor gave me a picture taken of it internally before its removal. It is framed and in the living room. No, it isn't really, but were you worried for just a moment?

It's funny now that I think about it, that while we were waiting in the lobby of the plastic surgery center, we were watching a home improvement show on TV. They were remodeling a home, tearing out old fixtures, and putting in new upgrades. A variation on a theme. My plastic surgeon is Dr. B. She comes with high recommendations from my general surgeon and others. I like her down-to-earth personality.

That visit was different than any other I have had. It included standing in front of a full-length mirror in nothing but undies while a woman I just met maneuvered my chest around, then to investigating a suitcase full of implants and playing with those, to having said woman take pictures of my nude chest. I laughed a little when she started pulling down the black screen that I would stand in front of for the pictures. She heard me and said she guessed I don't do that often, other than at home. I said I usually charge for those kinds of pictures, to which she replied that I was instead paying her. Touché doc!

The outcome of that visit was that I learned what will be done to rebuild my bra-fillers and picked out the materials. The doctor also told me that what she doesn't like about patients like me is that I have pretty boobs. Yeah, that's right. She said she prefers when women come in with ones that sag or don't look good, and she can make them better. I'm having to give up a nice set apparently. My favorite phrase of hers was, "God-made is always better than man-made." She told me she can't do what He does but can get close. So nice to have a doctor that understands who the ultimate creator is and doesn't feel she can take His place. I greatly appreciated that.

We also talked about another option for reconstruction that uses your own tissue to rebuild. That includes another surgery where they take from either your belly or back. She told me that I didn't have enough fat in either area to rebuild second base. In one day, I was told that I was a good candidate for surgery because I was young, then told that I have pretty boobs and that I don't have enough fat to build body parts with. It was a good day, all things considered.

So, here's a little side story about the plastic surgeon visit that I have only shared with a couple of privileged confidants, until now. When I was led into the exam room, the nurse pulled out a gown and asked that I remove everything except my underwear before putting it on. That sent a wave of panic down my spine as she left the room. I stood there paralyzed with my brain in high gear trying to figure out what to do. I looked at my husband and he knew why I was having a hard time. He just shook his head and gave me a sideways glance of shame. I swallowed my pride and went out to find the nurse. I got her aside and asked if I could just remove my top half and leave my pants on. She said that the doctor really needed me to have everything off, but I could keep my underwear on. That's when I whispered to her that I wasn't wearing any. It didn't much phase her. She said that it happens and handed me a plastic, sealed package with some silky little blue panties in it.

I had no idea when I was getting ready that morning that I was going to be handed a cancer diagnosis and end up with doctor visits, so I treated it like any other day. The doctors had fit me into their schedules, so I couldn't ask for other times and wasn't able to run home to adjust my attire. I hate panty lines and am not a fan of thong undies. I had found a style at Victoria's Secret that I liked and wasn't too bad, but I had discovered going commando on occasion to be a much more comfortable option. Okay, if I'm going to be truly honest, on more occasions than not. That day was no exception. I was horrified at the nurse's directions and didn't know what I was going to do. My husband, knowing my undergarment preference, was sending me vibes of, "I told you so!" I was reassured, though, when it seemed like no big deal, and I received the panty package from the nurse.

I thought I had mostly escaped a terribly awkward situation, but I was incorrect. After the plastic surgeon had completed the exam, she slyly asked if I was wearing their underwear. I sheepishly admitted that I was. When she asked why it was all I could do to keep it together and spit out that it was because I wasn't wearing any when I came in. I didn't die of embarrassment at that moment only because Dr. B. had already put me at ease, and we had a good rapport. Some levity was needed that day, but I didn't know it would come at the expense of my nether regions. I still giggle when I think about it. It's okay for you to laugh, too, that's why I'm telling you.

That was quite a noteworthy day. In a matter of hours, my and my family's lives had taken an uncertain turn. Now, I had to decide how and when to tell my boys.

The surgery will go like this: Dr. W. will make incisions across each breast and remove all the tissue possible including the nipples. They could be spared but doing so would leave a small amount of breast tissue and an area where cancer could grow again in the future. There is no point to keep them, as they would have no feeling after the fact anyway. The plastic surgeon will take care of the cosmetics later. Why leave avoidable risk? During the first part of the surgery, the nearest lymph node will also be removed and tested, at that time, for cancer cells. If any are found, another couple will be removed for testing. These results will help determine if additional treatment is needed after the surgery. Because the ultrasound showed the nodes to look clean, Dr. W. said he doesn't expect to find anything in them. There could be a surprise, but I'm going to go with no. When he has finished his part, Dr. B. will step in.

She will go behind the chest muscle and insert expanders on both sides. Since all the tissue is being removed, the implants must go behind the muscle, which will need to be stretched. A small amount of saline will be injected into the expanders. She will finish, close up and I'll spend the night in the hospital. Providing all goes as planned, I'll go home the next day with drains in each side. For the first week or so, I won't be able to do much, no lifting, no repetitive motions, just a lot of resting. Recovery will take between three and six weeks.

Over the following two to three months, I will visit Dr. B. every two weeks for additional saline injections. Each addition will help stretch the muscle and make pockets for the implants. As she put it, she'll keep pumping them up until I tell her to stop. This isn't about getting bigger boobs, it's about beating cancer and my future health, BUT, if I have to do this, I might as well get something out of it. Why not get the gift of defying gravity and the option of applying for a second job at Hooters for Christmas money.

The second surgery in the fall, will be outpatient and maybe two days off work. At that time, the expanders will be removed, and implants inserted. Nipples will also be reconstructed and later, pigment will be tattooed into them, as well as the surrounding area to represent the areola. It all seems kind of surreal when I think about it too much. I'm going to leave the hospital with everything removed from my chest and I'm assuming looking basically flat. Slowly, my chest will grow and change over the course of months, the whole time being smooth like a fashion doll. I have been a Barbie collector but never wanted my chest to look like hers. I'll actually be more like Growing Up Skipper. Skipper was Barbie's little sister. In the 70's they released a controversial version of her that went from a preteen to a young lady. She was flat-chested at first, but when you cranked her arm around once, she grew about an inch taller, and small boobs popped out. I still have my doll, I thought she was great.

I'm expecting that by the end of the year, things will be looking fairly normal. One of the unfortunate parts of this is the permanent loss of feeling and sensation in my chest. That's a bit of a bummer. It will be interesting to see how I react to all of this. I'm wondering what I'm going to feel the first time I see my chest, the incisions, my missing breasts, and later the scars. The pamphlet from the doctor suggests when you see yourself initially that you be alone and look first at your chest and then in the mirror. I'm anxious just thinking about it. This is the part I'm most worried about. I have faith that all cancer will be eliminated. I have watched three brave women in my family overcome this and know that it is treatable. My mom has gone near twenty years without additional issues after lumpectomies. My fear is more about the surgery itself and my new body. How am I going to feel about it? How is my husband going to look at me? How will he think of me? Will he still really be as attracted to me? I know he will say he will, but at first, I wonder. Walking through this together, I expect, will bring us closer, make us stronger and, I'm thinking, will bring an intimate bond that will be different, but in a positive way. It's a lot to face in any marriage, especially in your first year. I know that God deliberately put Eric in my life right at this time. Having him to walk through this with me was part of the plan. This is the second person that was placed in my life at just the right time during a life-changing event. I know there is a greater power at work here and that's how I know it will be okay.

One thing I have learned while navigating this new life is that things rarely go as expected during treatment. When I wrote this entry, I was pretty darn sure of how it was all going to go down. Looking at the entry now, the arrogance of my matter-of-fact, know-it-all attitude, makes me shake my head. Very little went as anticipated, except for the surgery itself. When graced with this diagnosis, one will fare best with the ability to roll with the punches and adjust preconceived notions. You need to be able to zig when you thought you were going to zag and be prepared to jump blindly into the abyss.

I was assured enough to think that I was going to have my new body by the end of the year. In fact, it took a couple of years to acquire an acceptable body. My second surgery did not take place in the fall, it didn't happen until early the next year and required much more than two days off work. The simple expander/implant exchange turned into a more involved surgery and recovery and the nipple situation was a whole other exciting experience.

SLEEPLESS IN SPRINGFIELD

So, I had cancer! I had been diagnosed, met with the doctors, had surgery planned and scheduled; the big stuff was done. Not hardly, bigger stuff was yet to come; I still had to tell my boys. I didn't have a clue of the best way to handle such a thing. I've always been rather straightforward with them, but with this, I was at a loss. We were the Three Musketeers, one unit to take on anything and everything that came our way.

When they were growing up, it tended to be just the three of us together more often than not. After the divorce, we grew that much closer, and they closed ranks to protect and support me the best that they could. I have always cherished the bond I have with my boys and didn't know how to approach this situation. The "sex talk" was awkward enough, how did I tell them that I had a disease that they had seen people die from? I have had to be strong for them in moments that I felt like I was breaking inside, and this was no different. I needed to summon all my courage, and strength, get my head on right and fill them in.

Eric and I had been careful of how we talked about things around the house between the time that I had been biopsied and was diagnosed. I didn't want to needlessly worry my boys, just in case it wasn't what it ended up being, but I also wanted to be fully armed with good information for them in the case that it was what we expected it to be. It was extremely hard to keep it together and act as if nothing was wrong around them during that time. It was truly going to be a relief to come clean and be able to breathe and feel the things that I needed to feel publicly and prepare for the impending surgery. There was one problem, though, Sam had gone away to camp. I had wanted to talk to them together, both for the comfort of us all being together, but, also so I would only have to go over it once. We had two more days until Sam would be home. It was only a couple of days, but I didn't know if I could keep up the charade that much longer. It had already been going on for a week and even two more days seemed like an eternity. I was going to try. I tried, I failed.

I couldn't hold it in any longer. I felt like a fraud around Jake, and it wasn't fair to him. As much as I didn't want one to hear before the other, I needed him to know, and it wasn't going to wait a couple more days. My kids are different in just about every single way; the things they like, the things they do, the way they dress, act, wear their hair, the way they process things, and the way they react. At the time, Jake was 18, and Sam, 14. Speaking to Jake on his own, I felt that I could walk into it more open than I could with Sam. Sometimes direct is best and that is how I forged ahead.

Jake was on the couch, so I sat down next to him with all the pamphlets and booklets that I had accumulated from the doctor visits and nonchalantly laid right into it. I told him that I had breast cancer and showed him in the pamphlets where it was and what it was and how we were going to treat it. He knew about all the women in the family who had dealt with this in the past. I reminded him that his Granny, my mom, had faced it twice and had come out just fine and that I was going to do the same. I know I was a little nervous and was talking fast, as I do when I'm anxious. He was calm and said that he knew it would be okay. He asked questions and was interested in all the details. I think there was some joking at that time about my replacement boobs. They became an instant source of comedy and remain so today. Jake likes to comment that, when he puts me in a home, I'll have the perkiest boobs there. The only problem that I have with that line of humor is that, at 18, he was already plotting to put me away.

Jake would become one of my closest confidants during treatment. He was home with me most often and we spent a lot of time talking about things that might not have come up as much with others. He wanted to know everything about my surgeries and what was going on with my healing. He even joined me in watching hours of the reality TV show, *Botched*, in preparation for surgery. If you are unfamiliar, the show features two Beverly Hills plastic surgeons who fix procedures that have been "botched". Each show typically features a nose job, a boob job, and one crazy situation that they usually opt not to do anything for because the person is either addicted to plastic surgery, has unreal expectations, is on the verge of destroying their appearance or body structure with more surgery or is just plain off their rocker. In seeing so many breast surgeries, I was able to get a good idea of what I was heading for on the reconstructive side. I saw several episodes where they worked on breast cancer survivors who had unfortunate reconstruction. It was entertaining, educational, and helped put me at ease.

When I picked Sam up from camp on Friday, I put on my bravest face and pulled out my finest acting skills to function as if nothing was out of the ordinary. After gathering up luggage, bedding, and a week's worth of dirty laundry, some quick "how are ya's" and "see ya laters" to his buddies, we were in the car. The drive home was filled with conversation about the events of his week. I was listening, but also working to discern how and when I would bring up to Sam the developments of my week. As it often is with kids, fun never lasts long enough. After a week of hanging out together, some of the guys wanted to prolong it and, before I knew it, Sam was off to his buddy's house for the night. I couldn't tell him before he left, so the charade continued.

I had a small window of time on Saturday to talk to him in between his engagements. My youngest child has always had a much fuller social calendar than myself. I could have probably approached the whole thing in a better manner, but I couldn't let another day go by. I remember that he was sitting at the kitchen counter eating when I sat down next to him to talk.

I laid it out, I had cancer, but it was small, I would have surgery, and everything would be okay. He looked at me with tears in his eyes, not believing the end of my statement. I assured him that I was going to be fine. I hugged him as he started to break down to give reassurance that I wasn't going anywhere just yet. His doubt came from the fact that he had just seen the movie, *A Fault in Our Stars*, two times in a short period. He was 14 and there were girls involved, which explained why he twice saw a movie that he, otherwise, wouldn't have likely seen at all. As always, timing is everything. I stressed that I was going to be okay, but he said that's what they thought in the movie, too, but then things weren't okay.

I reminded him that it was only a movie and that my mom had breast cancer twice, which was treated successfully, and she was doing great 20 years later. After we sat there for a bit, it seemed I had been able to convince him that it really was going to be fine. He went on to another friend's house that afternoon but returned home short of spending the night, as had been planned. I felt awful knowing that worry over our talk was the most feasible reason for his early return.

Sam settled into acceptance of what was happening. What else could he do? It was what it was, nothing could change that. I don't know what he thought on his own, but we went about our business with the cancer thing in the background. Unlike, Jake, Sam didn't want to talk about it. He didn't want to see pictures or get descriptive details of what was going to take place in surgery. I assume that was partly due to his age and partly due to underlying fear of the whole thing. There was close to a month before my surgery, until then, we could all only wonder what was to come.

There would be one more time that summer that a movie would provide the backdrop for a poignant shared moment between Sam and me. It was after my surgery that the boys and I went to see the movie, *Guardians of the Galaxy*. When you're a boy mom, you play with action figures and learn all the superheroes and await their movies. Mostly you don't mind, because, let's face it, the filmmakers know how to cast for those parts and their choices are not hard to look at. I get nearly as excited as my kids for the new Marvel movies and that one was no different. We had no idea, however, what was to come at the beginning of the movie.

Spoiler alert here, but, honestly, if you haven't seen this movie by now, you're not a true fan of the comics and this reveal likely won't matter to you. The movie starts with the hero as a child in the hall of a hospital. He is led in to see his mother who is lying in the hospital bed looking ill and frail with her bald head exposed. It's not hard to decipher that she is dying of cancer. Perfect! Just what we needed to see. This plot point is important to the movie and its sequel, but not what we needed that summer. I cry at movies. Most times, I'm able to control the tears that well up in my eyes and extinguish the few that escape before they travel down my face. That was not the case with this one. The tears just kept coming. I wiped them away as fast I could and stared straight ahead trying to wish away the water, but I couldn't stop them. Jake squeezed my hand to say that it was okay. I looked out the side of my eye at Sam to see him wiping away at moist eyes, as well. There was a palpable, somber feeling emanating from the chair next to me. Thankfully, the movie quickly moved into comedy and has a great soundtrack that helped lift us out of that moment. Once again, timing!

INVASION OF THE BOOBIE SNATCHERS

August 6, 2014

Day before surgery

Good morning! Thought for the day: "You gain strength, courage, and confidence by every experience in which you really stop to look fear in the face. You are able to say to yourself, 'I have lived through this horror. I can take the next thing that comes along."- Eleanor Roosevelt.

It's funny, I posted that to my Facebook page on the way into work this morning; when I got there, my desk had been decorated with signs and inspirational quotes and that was one of them. I enjoy my job for many reasons, but the main one is the people that I work with. Today, in addition to my workspace being thoughtfully decorated, the office ladies wore pink for me. I'm employed by a great company filled with wonderful people! My work support system extends up to the corporate office to those there with who I communicate often. Scheels is a family, my second family. I have such a large community of encouragement and so many prayers surrounding me right now, I know I'm well covered!

I left a sign at my desk saying "Out for Repair – See you in September" with a pink, breast cancer ribbon on it and off I went. I would return at the end of September.

August 7, 2014 (5:58 am)

It's B-Day! That's Boob Day, as this has been dubbed by my office mate. We are on the way to the hospital. I'm not too nervous. Didn't sleep much, so I'm just tired. Ready to wake up in recovery on the other side of this. Interesting emotions as I stood looking at my naked chest in the mirror before showering this morning. Said goodbye to The Girls. Not gonna lie, it's a bit surreal to know they're not going to be there when I wake up. Looking down a little farther near my hip at my pink ribbon tattoo reminds me that this is my destiny, part of my family inheritance, such as it is. I'm joining six other women in my family in this and a huge number out there who I've never met, but who I'm now connected to through this sisterhood. I know it's going to be fine, and the weight of worry will be off my shoulders when it is all said and done. I have complete faith in my doctors and in knowing that God has me taken care of. Love to you all and we'll talk soon!

I was eerily calm that morning, being only slightly anxious about the surgery, as it was a new experience for me. I was more in the mode of just getting it done and moving forward. Previous life adventures have forged in me a "this is what's happening now, no option but to go with it and seek the best from it" kind of attitude in situations like this. When there are obstacles that you cannot eliminate, you do what must be done to overcome them, there's really no other choice. After the initial shock and then acceptance of my diagnosis, I had resolved to face the cancer in my chest head-on and obliterate it with whatever steps necessary.

I did have a moment with my girls that morning. They had been with me for 44 years and I realized that I had largely taken them for granted. We were mere hours from parting, and they deserved some acknowledgment. It felt a bit like anticipating the impending death of a couple of dear friends. It almost seemed like a moment for a eulogy. *"I am honored and privileged to have been acquainted with left boob and right boob for my entire life. They have been constant companions and I would like to thank them for enhancing my shirts whenever possible. It is with great sadness that I say goodbye to my friends and wish them Godspeed as they move on to a better place where they can run and frolic tumor and cancer-free."* Or something like that. I took a picture for posterity and bid them adieu before showering with the sterile smelling, red, antiseptic, pre-surgery soap. Not the most luxurious last lathering for them I suppose but I doubt that they thought anything of it.

Here's a bit of a side note about the pink ribbon tattoo mentioned in this post. Around the time I turned 40, I started thinking seriously about getting a tattoo. I was in the process of divorcing and working on the "new me", the stronger version of the woman I had been, one who took the initiative to do what she wanted and break out of the shell she had been living in. I had been toying around with the idea of getting a pink ribbon somewhere in memory and honor of my family members, specifically my grandmother and my mom, but hadn't been ready to pull the trigger on it. I kept it in the back of my mind.

It would be another year before it was time. I had a cousin visiting from California, so a group of family got together to go out and hang out a bit. Adult beverages were consumed and the conversation at the table turned to my cousin's tattoos and the Asian symbol on the back of her neck. She said that it meant family. Another cousin commented that he liked it and that it would be cool to go as a group and get that same tattoo. It was a fun idea. I mentioned before that I have a large extended family and I wasn't kidding. There are hordes of us cousins, but we are a close-knit group and most of us live in the same area. However, we didn't see our cousin, Michelle, very often since she was living in Cali. It would be something special to unite us. I said that I had been wanting to get a tattoo and was in, but I wanted a pink ribbon, instead. Michelle said she would get the same and two of the guys settled on getting the family symbol. We were going to do it the next day.

That next day, we got together and the four of us went to get inked. The three of us here in town were tattoo virgins, so it was quite an experience, but one that bonds us four in a unique way. Tony got the family symbol on the inside of his arm and John on his outer leg. I got a pink ribbon with a halo, added for my grandma, near my right hip and Michelle added a pink ribbon to the inside of her wrist. When I left the house that day, I told my boys that I was going to hang out with the family but didn't say what I would be doing. Telling my teenage sons that their 41-year-old mom got tattooed was funny. My oldest didn't think much of it, but my youngest was a bit in shock. How could I do that? What? Why? He was unaware of just how cool his old mom was. I think he was a little embarrassed but has since accepted it.

At the time of our inking, none of us knew that the pink ribbons that Michelle and I got that night would come to honor her mom, as well, just a couple of years later. Prior to my diagnosis, my Aunt Joyce would fight and lose a brutal battle with breast cancer.

The point of sharing the tattoo story is to share this one. The next morning, I was still reeling at the events of the day before. I had to call my closest girlfriend, Jami, and tell her what I had done. I relayed the whole story about my two male cousins getting the family symbol and where and how Michelle and I got the pink ribbon and all the details. She couldn't believe it and laughed along as I blurted it all out. Now, here's the amazing part of this tale: Late that night, she called me up. Jami started telling me about the trivia night that she had gone to with friends. It seemed that her friend invited her, and the husband invited one of his friends. They were sitting at the table and the husband's friend was telling them how he had gone the night before with a few of his cousins to get his first tattoo. He and another had gotten the symbol for family that he showed them on his leg. The picture became clear, and Jami asked him who his cousin was. You guessed it, it was my cousin, John. Of all the people who could have been there, the stars had to align just perfectly for that to happen. They hit it off and the rest is now history.

They have been married for several years and my best girlfriend is also family and a pink ribbon tied it all together. She was among the first that I told of my diagnosis and has been a huge part of my support system. Funny how things like that come around. Maybe it would have all turned out the same if she hadn't known he was my cousin that night, but maybe not. There was, likely, a bit more comfort in knowing someone that he was close to that she was also close to and could get good intel from. I like to think that the whole thing was fate sprinkled with a little pink.

(9:13 am)

Final post before heading to surgery

Just came down from getting shot up in Nuclear Med. They injected me with something to light up the sentinel lymph node. I asked the guy if it would make my boob glow. He said it would, but we were disappointed when we turned out the lights and it didn't. Was hoping to have a little rave party, courtesy of my light-up chest. (Okay, so he said, "No", it wouldn't do that, but it was a fun thought.)

It was dreary when we checked in early that morning and it proceeded to storm quite heavily. I saw my docs soon after getting settled and was then hooked up to an IV.

My plastic surgeon wanted to be sure that we were on the same page and asked a final time if we were removing everything, including the nipples. Yes, take my nips, please. In case you are wondering from the previous discussion about what might be done with them, I did ask her if I could keep them. Of course, the answer was a resounding, "NO!" Apparently, you are no longer allowed to keep any excised body parts. Just like back in school, someone along the way messed up and ruined that for everyone. I didn't actually want them, but I had to ask. I enjoyed seeing the look of disbelief on Eric's face of the things that would come out of my mouth, and I also enjoy keeping people on their toes.

The surgery would be performed in the day surgery area of the Baylis Building, which is attached to the hospital. It feels a bit more relaxed, so it wasn't as daunting to check in to. For the nuclear injection, though, I was wheeled over to an area of the actual hospital and put in a small room with the young man who would shoot me up with radioactive dye. The room was white and cold, and you could hear the thunder outside.

I was starting to feel a little nervous about the looming events of the day. The technician was very respectful and quiet and gentle when explaining what was going to happen. There was an empathetic feeling in the air. It was making me anxious, so I needed to break the ice and let him know that I wasn't fragile and that I was okay with my situation and what was to come. I was also trying to convince myself of that and get my thought processes back on track. When I asked about my boob glowing, it lightened the mood, and then it was all smooth from there.

The dye would be injected slowly near the site of cancer. He said that it might burn. It did. I think I shed a couple of tears. They weren't due to the pain of the injection or the dye searing through my vein, but to the reality of the process that this procedure was the start of. There were fleeting moments that morning and before when the gravity of my reality would set in. I would acknowledge those moments, wallow in them for a minute and then kick them aside as best I could. Forward was the only direction to go.

Once the injection was completed, the dye would require an hour to travel through the lymph system and light the path to the sentinel, or closest, lymph node. That lymph node would be identified during surgery, removed, and biopsied for any signs of cancer cells. If no cancer cells are found in that node, the assumption is the cancer has not spread into the lymphatic system and other places in the body. I was moved from the small room where we had been into the CT room to wait out my hour. It was a much larger room, of course, to house the huge Cat Scan machine. One wall was windows looking into an adjoining room where the techs were. There was a TV overhead to watch while waiting out the time, however, the storm had taken out the reception, so the same show was on every channel, snow. I was in another cold room with only hard surfaces and uncomfortable chairs for an hour with nothing to read or watch. It was a long wait.

It was early in the morning, and I had not had much sleep. I was so tired and, with nothing else to do but sit and stare around the bleak room, I was starting to nod off. I tried to get comfy sitting up in the hard chair with my head back, thinking I could catch a nap, then I became self-conscious and fought it. I was aware of the likelihood that, if I fell asleep, my mouth would pop open and I would snore, because that is how I roll. Wait, I forgot about the drooling. Yeah, it's not always a pretty sight when I sleep, I'm afraid. That is the reason that I was extra cautious back in my school days about falling asleep in class, I feared snoring. That would have been an event that I probably wouldn't have walked away from unscathed. There was a time or two in high school Study Hall that I did nap a bit with my head on my desk. I would wake up with a puddle of drool under me and my hair stuck in it across the side of my face, but, to my knowledge, I didn't snore, at least not enough to be heard over anyone else asleep in that class. At any rate, there in the CT room, I was on display, as it was, due to the large glass wall leading into the other room. Even though I had no makeup on, was in an unattractive, oversized hospital gown, was 44 and about to become boobless, I was concerned about the cute, young med techs seeing me sleeping. How silly! That vanity would be diminished in the months to come, as chemo would strip things away from me, but at that moment, I was still firmly entrenched in it.

I finally couldn't take it any longer and decided to lay down on the CT table with the cotton hospital blanket and try to catch a few winks. My face would be out of their line of sight, for the most part, and I was getting to the point that I no longer cared. You can only sit with your thoughts on a day like that for so long before you need to try to escape from them. I started out flat on my back, then went from one side to the other. I had my legs bent and then straight, hand under head, then down at my side. The hard CT table wasn't conducive to sleep, but I think I may have dozed off for a few minutes.

Finally, the hour was up, and my rave party buddy came in to do the CT. The point was to check and be sure that the dye had made it to its destination and would show the lymphatic path that they were after. It was quick, it was done and off I went for a total double mastectomy.

My husband posted updates throughout the day as he received them.

August 7, 2014 (9:48 am)

Lisa has been taken back to the operating room. Surgery to begin in about 30 minutes. It should take 3-4 hours. I will update again when I hear from the doctor, but from what I can gather, they do not foresee any problems.

(11:50 am)

The doctor just came out to let me know that everything went as planned. All tissue was removed, and the lymph node was tested and came back clean, so no worries there. She still has another hour or so while the reconstructive surgeon does her part, but then she will be in recovery before being moved over to Memorial.

(2:54 pm)

Lisa is awake and alert and has been moved to her room.

(4:40 pm)

The brave gal is pretty sore but handling everything well and is in good spirits. Unfortunately, she isn't so out of it that I can take advantage. I told her that I was hoping to get a good YouTube quality video of some loopy behavior. Oh well.

About nine hours after arriving at the hospital, it was over, and I was settled into a private room. I wasn't out of my mind enough to satisfy Eric's wicked sense of humor, but I was still a bit foggy. I honestly have only a few memories of that evening. My cousin and his now-wife, my close friend who you met earlier in the tattoo story, paid a visit and I was able to talk with them for a few minutes. My sons and mom and stepsons also visited shortly after surgery, but I entirely slept through their time. I was so upset to find out that they had been there, and I didn't know it. When I asked my husband why he didn't wake me, he said that I needed the rest. I had been asleep most of the day, I could have withstood a little time awake with my visitors. My oldest son enjoyed that I was sleeping because my previously mentioned tendency was on display; my mouth was open, and I was snoring. He took pictures, that he was quite proud of, but was later convinced to delete.

I know that I ate something for dinner but have no idea what it was. What I do remember clearly, though, is the push to use the bathroom. The nurses are very serious about making sure that your plumbing is working properly before even thinking about going home, and I could not go. Getting out of bed was difficult due to not being able to use my arms, so I needed help up and into the bathroom. Then, of course, I had had several hours of anesthesia, so they didn't want me in there alone. The bathroom was behind a curtain rather than a door, so the nurses were okay with me being there unassisted, but only with the curtain open and them in the big room. My husband was also in the room. We had only been married nine months, we weren't quite to the shared bathroom experience stage, which we never reached, that was awkward. It took several tries and extended time sitting on the porcelain throne to achieve success. Crazy as it is, that's the most vivid memory from the night after one of my life's biggest events.

(After napping, eating, and bathroom time, I hopped online to check what was happening on my Facebook page and put up a new post that wasn't the most coherent.)

August 8 (12:28 am)

Lying here tonight with a sense of relief. Relieved went well and that the mode *(node)* was clean. Relieved that surgery went well that the mode *(node)* didn't show any cancer cells. Best news all day. *(Edit: I just saw how grammatically terrible this post is. I was having difficulty updating on my phone. The Vicodin is making my vision a little blurry and on the small phone screen, I had double vision. Almost like drunk texting, I think.)*

When I finally came around and had time to process where I was and what had happened that day, it felt like some kind of dream. That was my first surgery, and it was a doozy. The only thing I wanted to know was if the lymph node was clean. In a Vicodin haze, I kept asking about that and, once I got clarity, I felt an immense relief wash over me. That was a victory!

AFTER THE BOOBS ARE GONE

August 9, 2014

I am home. Was released late yesterday afternoon. It was nice to get settled into my spot on the couch. It's a genuinely comfortable reclining couch and I'm set up with plenty of pillows and blankets. I have a basket on the table next to me holding my meds, some magazines, a book, hand lotion, hand sanitizer, lip balm, my chargers, and some Tums. Also, have a souvenir back scratcher from the Ozarks. You know the type, plastic with a little hand on the end. The kind you would get at a roadside Stuckey's. I've come close to throwing it out in the past, so glad I didn't. Pain meds are making me itch. I also have three wonderful guys at my beck and call. Everything I need right now is close at hand. The other essential for my recuperation is on my lap. Our sweet little one-eyed cat, Zazu, took her spot on my lap last night and has stayed. She is currently sporting a lovely plastic cone around her head due to an issue in the area of the missing eye, so here we sit looking pathetic together. She knows when I need a little extra love and is happy to provide it.

My upper body is wrapped tightly, so I haven't gotten a look at the incisions, but just seeing myself in the bandages is odd. My chest is flatter than flat. I have the profile of a nine-year-old girl. Like I talked about before the surgery, I'm feeling like a Growing Up Skipper doll, pre-arm cranking. That's where I am right now, except instead of cranking my arm, it will be a series of saline injections that will create my starter boobs. The hardest part was over, now let the healing begin!

I had set up my recuperation spot on the couch so that coming home would be as easy as possible. Some online searching and significant thought helped me anticipate the main items that would be good to have on the side table close at hand. My self-designated area on the couch included both *Spider-Man* and *Pirates of the Caribbean* sheets leftover from the boys' childhood bedding, as well as a couple of soft, fuzzy blankets and an array of pillows. That would be my home for several weeks after that surgery and even more with other surgeries to come. It was the perfect spot to heal in.

I must admit to a bit of a love affair with my couch, which was increased ten-fold over several phases of surgery recuperation. Little did I know when I bought the four-piece sectional the year after becoming suddenly single, that it would fill such a need just a few years later. I had a tax refund windfall that year and decided to treat myself to new furniture. I figured I was due after fifteen years with the same furnishings that were purchased when moving into the house. I bought a small sectional, another side sofa and a nice dining room table and chair set. It would be the most expensive single purchase that I had made entirely on my own, ever, and I didn't take it lightly. It was actual adulting.

I went to the furniture store at least three times and looked over and over. When I decided what I wanted, I was very thoughtful about being sure that it would fit. Our living room is quite narrow and has odd walls that lend themselves to limited furniture setups. I took measurements of each available section of couch, went home, and taped it out on the floor to see what configuration would fit. It was a big deal. It was a good chunk of money, and I couldn't afford to waste it. I can confidently say that the reclining couch is one of my favorite things in the house, aside from the living creatures, of course. It is over-stuffed ultra-suede with two recliners and a chaise lounge divided by a small storage section and super comfy! I am quite passionate about my couch, can you tell? It's a good thing, since the combined time that I lived on that couch in 2014 and the years after, easily totaled several months. My process for deciding on the couch illustrates how I tend to approach big things in my life. I do a lot of mulling over, reading reviews, and comparing similar items before going ahead with pricey or important purchases, booking a hotel room, finding a new restaurant to eat at when traveling, or choosing how to tackle a situation. Decisions to be made after that initial surgery would be approached with the same amount of mindfulness. Those decisions were, by far, some of the most important that I would ever have to make. There are many important choices to be made in breast cancer treatment that should be tackled with no less than the thought that went into buying my couch.

Zazu the cat came to live with us only a few months earlier. We adopted her on Mother's Day, 2014. Jake and I had been volunteering at a feline shelter in the area. Once a week, we would clean a few of the rooms, feed the cats, and spend time playing with them. We came to know several of them very well. The first night there, as I was bent over scooping a litter box, I felt something land on my back. A tortoiseshell cat had jumped down from a hanging shelf right onto me. She promptly laid down and made herself comfortable. I wasn't quite sure what to do with that right then. Jake helped to remove her, and we went about our business. That particular room seemed to be the most active and the little tortie with one eye was the ringleader. We would come in to find cat trees knocked over, towels pulled down off the shelves, and general chaos. She talked to us emphatically while we were there and often tried to make a run for it. I became quite fond of the big personality in the little cat body. We fell in love with her.

I knew that we had to adopt that sassy little girl, but we had a grouchy senior cat at home, and I needed to figure out the best way to add her to our family without upsetting him too much. I made my intentions to adopt her known to the shelter caretaker. Zazu was eight years old at the time. Being an older cat, she had not been taken out to any adoption events during the year that she had lived there. That being the case and the shelter knowing that we wanted her, I felt we had some time to work out a transition. Monday morning, a week later, I was told by my friend who took care of the shelter cats, that Zazu had been taken to an adoption event over the weekend, but she was still at the store, and she didn't think she had been adopted. I called the people in charge right away only to find out that adoption papers had been filled out on her, but she hadn't been picked up yet. I explained that we had planned to adopt her and made that known, but all they could do was apologize. Jake and I were heartbroken. She had slipped right through our fingers. At the end of the week, I received a call from the shelter. The adoption wasn't completed, the family never claimed her. They were holding her for us if we still wanted her. I couldn't believe it! I filled out the paperwork and Zazu moved into her new home with us on Mother's Day. A perfect example of a seemingly hopeless situation turning into a positive and at just the right time; a recurring theme in my life. As I mentioned in my post, our sweet little Zazzy became my constant companion and showered me with love three months later during my first surgery and the subsequent ones.

I was completely wrong about one thing in this post; the hardest part was nowhere near over. I had no idea what challenges were to come.

August 10, 2014

Feeling more human than I have in days. Getting my hair washed has made all the difference. I have an incredible home nurse who is super cute, as well! Eric has been so wonderful! When we made our wedding vows just nine and a half months ago, neither of us expected the "in sickness" possibility to show up so soon and in such a way. Without hesitation, he has jumped in and done everything needed. He has become an expert at stripping and emptying the drains, as well as measuring and logging the output. He has mastered the sponge bath and found out that he can wash, comb and dry long hair. Anything I need, he is right there with it. I cannot express my gratitude enough for this amazing man. I can't imagine how much harder this would be without him. God put him in my life at the right time, it was no accident. It's a lot for our newlywed year but surviving this will make us unstoppable.

This is as good a place as any to mention that not all fairy tales have a happy ending. When I wrote that post and the subsequent ones on the blog, I truly felt that we were creating a bond that couldn't be broken but it didn't quite work out that way. In real-time, we are now separated. In the months following publication, we will likely be divorced. This has nothing to do with our cancer experience and everything to do with us going in different directions and needing and wanting different things. That doesn't negate the fact that Eric stepped in when I needed him the most and did everything that he physically could to help me. I will always be grateful and, for that, and he will maintain a special place in my heart.

The emotions expressed in the posts are true to what was happening at the time. As I have said before and will mention again, more than once before this book is completed, the people that we need are dropped into our lives exactly at the times that we need them. Some of those people are not meant to stay forever, but that doesn't alter their importance. Eric is an integral part of my journey and that will always be so. I also feel there is a reason that I was placed in his life, and the near eleven years we spent together were a benefit to us both.

August 11, 2014 (9:00 am)

It's 9:00 and I am ready for the day. I have been washed up and changed into clean clothes, had some oatmeal for breakfast accompanied by a nice dose of Vicodin, and am nestled comfortably on the couch among a group of pillows with ice packs under my arms and a warm kitty curled up on my lap, small comforts make this all easier. Four days in and Eric and I have settled into this routine. I haven't cried much in the course of all of this, but this morning while getting cleaned up, a wave of emotion overtook me. There was just something about the moment that struck me. I was standing there mostly naked as my husband so gently and lovingly washed my neck, shoulders, and arms. I say, mostly naked because my chest is wrapped tightly in a large ace bandage emphasizing the flat landscape with a tube coming from each side attached to a bulb drain. These are pinned up to the bandage, it's rather sci-fi looking. Part of the morning routine is emptying these drains and measuring the output. I think that part of it is what brought about my tears. For me, this whole production is temporary, but I thought for a moment about those who do this daily on a continual basis. Knowing that Eric would do this for me day after day for as long as needed, brought up a feeling that I can't even put into words; a feeling of love like none other. It was very overwhelming.

When unexpected things happen in life, you adjust and figure out how to deal with them the best you can. What other choice do you have? None, really. Eric and I adjusted and figured out how to make things work smoothly. We quickly created a routine for morning and night. It was a little odd having him wash me, not that he hadn't done that before, but the circumstances had certainly been different. This time, there was no possibility of things becoming amorous. There could be no showers until the drains were out, so it was strictly sink bathing for that first week. I remember how gentle he was the first day that he cleaned me up. I think he was afraid of hurting me, but anything that could be hurt was securely covered. I'm sure it was a bit scary for him, but that subsided soon enough. When I told him that he was going to have to wash and brush my long hair, he was concerned but went for it. I hung my head over the kitchen sink for the shampooing and he mastered it well enough that I was presentable.

The worst part of the process, by far, was emptying the drains. I had two bulb drains. Each had to be stripped and emptied twice a day. The blood and fluid needed to be poured into a marked container and measured in the morning and again at night. The measurements were recorded and reported to the doctor to determine the extent of drainage and when it had decreased enough to eliminate the grenade-shaped, soft plastic units hanging out of me. Stripping them entailed pinching the tube exiting my body then running those pinched fingers down the length of the tube to get all the liquid out and clear any clots that might block it up. It was a bit of a gross process, but we got used to it and it became part of the routine.

The breast cancer ride is an absolute emotional roller coaster, and you never know when it is going to throw you for a loop. As I watched my husband run the washcloth down my neck, across my shoulder, down my arm, and then under my arm and across the top of the tight chest bandage for the fourth day in a row, I couldn't keep it together. I was overcome with his love and care and the thought of what it would be like if that was our reality for the rest of our days and a sadness knowing that there are couples who have that existence. It was too much to contain. When I think about it now, that same feeling materializes. It was a powerful experience.

(11:13 pm)

Cleaned up and ready for bed. The nighttime routine is not quite as much as the morning. Drains are emptied and output measured and recorded, face is washed, teeth brushed, clothes changed. I found a nightgown that I could slip on feet first. It has a tube top and then flows freely from there. Funny, because I have these bulb drains hanging on each side just above my waist, in this gown the way they are hanging under the material, it looks like I have a couple of pretty saggy gals. It reminded me of the Maxine character from the greeting card world. Gave Eric and me both a chuckle. Sagging is not something that I will have to worry about in the future. Bonus! Perky will be the name of the game.

Settled in now with fresh ice in my ice packs and ice water on the table, meds taken, pillows arranged, covers in place, phone and remote at hand. I just need my feline companion to take her place on my lap and I'm ready for a full night of resting up for the next full day of resting up.

From the beginning, I was able to move my arms to the point that I could handle my own bathroom needs and wash areas to the immediate south of the equator. The doctor had told me to keep my arms as still as possible and mostly down by my sides. The more movement, the more drainage, the more drainage, the longer the drains would be in. My goal was to have them out at my first follow-up appointment, so I mostly did as I was told. I would assist in getting myself cleaned up but accepted and appreciated the help that I received in the areas that I needed it.

One thing that I could not do without pain, however, was push down with my hands and put pressure on my arms. That made getting up from the couch a bit difficult. I hadn't thought that in the month between diagnosis and surgery, I should have been focusing on strengthening my core. That would have aided in getting to a standing position from sitting without pushing off. To get up, I needed help. One of my lovely male nurses would come and help pull me forward by putting their arms under my arms, with hands around the back to lift. It took a little practice, but they all mastered the pull and lift. At night, though, my nurses went off shift and I was left to my own devices.

The reclining couch was amazing for resting and keeping my feet up, but a real booger to get up from on my own in the middle of the night. Once reclined, you need to push your bottom back to sit forward and then push down the foot extension in order to stand. This is rather easy to accomplish when you have your hands and arms to assist in getting upright, but not so much without. I imagine that it would have been quite the sight to watch me scoot my way down to where I could get enough weight on the foot extension to lower my feet to the floor, roll onto my side and lean my body enough on the edge of the couch seat next to me to stand up. I will admit to a little bit of grunting and cursing and a few tears the first couple of evenings. I am glad that no one saw the spectacle that was me getting up to use the bathroom in the wee hours of those nights. The cat witnessed it, but she never mentioned it to anyone. I do think I heard her snicker a few times, but I could have imagined that. The least she could have done was lend a paw. I eventually became proficient in the scoot, roll, and stand and the nights got better.

August 12, 2014

It was nice to have my mom come out today and wash my hair and help me clean up. No matter how old you get, there's nothing like your momma's care. Also, a bit of special bonding since she has been down this road herself. We had the same cancers in the same place and at the same age; her first time, anyway. She faced it twice, both times treated with lumpectomy, but we had the same drain situations. I am honored to be so much like my mom. This isn't necessarily something I had hoped to have in common, but I will proudly share the name of Survivor with her. Love you, Mom!

My mother is the strongest person that I know. She has consistently held things together and has been the model of how to weather any storm with grace and success. I'm not saying that I have always been graceful or successful in handling my stuff, but I have seen up close how it should be and can be done. Raising me on her own, without fail, she met my needs and did what was best for me even in the face of immense personal trials. She is the example that I look to when in similar situations. Our breast cancer battles were only slightly comparable but having seen her defeat it, twice, I knew I could prevail.

CLOUDY WITH A CHANCE OF MEATBALLS AND CHICKEN AND LASAGNA AND PIE AND...

August 13, 2014

It's been almost a week since my surgery. Can't believe it has passed so quickly! I am surprised at how little pain I have. I didn't know what to expect, but I expected a lot more pain. I'm thankful that there has been less, for sure. The worst of it was in getting up just after surgery and moving around. Beyond that, I would say it's been mostly discomfort. There is pressure across my chest. I have heard it described as an elephant sitting on your chest or a semi parked on it. I agree with both. The bandage on my chest is bothering me the most; it is so tight and uncomfortable. Last night I wasn't feeling too awesome. It was probably the first time that I was hurting a bit; having some shots of pain on my chest and it was aching under my arms. I was annoyed for no apparent reason. Today is better except for the tightness.

My left underarm is numb where the lymph node was removed. That feels weird. I got a peek under my arms today when I was cleaning up and it was scary. Let's just say that I'm not the Bohemian type, I prefer to have bare underarms. I tried shaving with my electric razor without much success. Oh well, guess I'll embrace the European way for now. The drainage has slowed considerably and I'm hoping to have the drains out on Friday. I'm getting a bit tired of lying around, but I can tell when I've been up too much, and I know my body needs the rest. I'm feeling better every day things are healing.

This journey is moving forward, and I am thankful that things are going well. I'm also blessed with so many wonderful people who are checking on me. I am surrounded by beautiful cards and flowers, and we are having great meals delivered every night. One of the best parts is getting my kids to do anything I want. They are checking on me frequently and are quick to do whatever I ask. Last night, Eric was smacking around on some ice to fill my ice packs when Sam ran upstairs and came to me asking what I needed. I told him I didn't need anything. He heard the banging and thought it was me trying to get his attention. I laughed but was impressed that he was so quick to respond.

I was getting tired of resting, but I was tired and so, I was resting. I knew that I needed the downtime to heal and facilitate the removal of the drains, but it was starting to wear on me. I didn't have the energy to do much of anything and there wasn't much I could do anyway. The tightness of the bandage and the compression of the expanders on the inside were stifling. Little did I know how much worse that crushing feeling was going to become in time. I was being well taken care of; my guys were very attentive. Every time someone got up to leave the room or pass by, they asked if I needed anything. The main thing that I needed regularly was my ice packs switched out. I kept ice packs under both arms at all times. That wasn't mandated but highly suggested, at least in the early days. I became a huge fan, and they became a near-constant in the weeks after surgery. Those packs helped keep the swelling down and just felt so darn good. Never underestimate the power of ice!

Many of the visitors that I had that first week came bearing the gift of food. My cousin had set up a meal train for us and it was filled for every available meal. As humans, we often equate food with love and comfort. We gather with friends and family to share meals to celebrate, to bond, to mourn, and sometimes just to fill a need, but there is often that feeling of community around a meal. We were certainly blessed with community that week and for several more weeks surrounding the initial surgery and the next. I enjoyed having face-to-face time with others outside of my homeboys who were caring for me. It was nice to see people that I hadn't recently seen or who had never been to our home. We were all thankful for the food.

I'm sure that Eric was glad to not have to come up with and prepare all the meals and it was good that we didn't have to rely on fast food or takeout. We were fed well and had a wide variety to choose from. It became a thing to wonder or guess what might be for dinner. There was so much food! Too much food! I can never thank those who brought meals to us enough; their love was absorbed and consumed, but sometimes kindness can be overwhelming. In those weeks, our cups and bowls, pans, and fridge runneth over. It got to be a bit too much. Our benefactors were generous, and the meals were large, most often coming complete with sides and dessert. We couldn't eat all of any of them in one sitting. We had leftovers on top of leftovers. It became a race against time to eat everything. The abundance of food became comical at a point. We didn't want to throw anything out, but it was impossible to ingest it all. Don't think for one minute that I am looking a gift horse in the mouth, because that is not at all the case. I know that those meals took time and money and were an immeasurable gift and help to us and we appreciated every bite, however, a lesson was learned. The next time that meals were organized, we spread them out a bit more and filled them in with leftovers and takeout. I will also implement what I learned if I find myself delivering a meal. Just a little handy tip.

In case you are wondering about the underarm situation they are still numb, especially on the lymph node side. It is a strange sensation and shaving continues to be a challenge. Without looking in a mirror, which most don't have in the shower, it's difficult to know where the razor is traveling when you can't feel it. One of many small things that connect us pink survivors.

August 14, 2014 (10:46 am)

I had the strangest dream early this morning. I went to the salon for a makeover and got my hair dyed red. Went back to sleep and dreamt that I was at the hospital, and they cut my boobs off. Then I woke up and... AWWW...NUTS!!! Eric told me I could dye my hair red if I wanted. I reminded him that I do have a red wig in the basement. It was from a Little Red Riding Hood Halloween costume.

(3:30 pm)

Have been taking it very easy today. I overdid it a bit

yesterday and my body told me so. I'm going to force myself to stay down and heal completely. My cat is helping there. When she settles in on my lap, she makes it so I can't get up. This morning I had to text Sam to come and move her so that I could go to the bathroom. Every time I tried to move her, she just snuggled in more. She knows what I need to do. I need to become cat-like and just lay around; sleep a little, stretch out, turn around, lay down and then sleep some more. I'm feeling good emotionally, too. Getting rid of a couple of body parts that you have come to know, and love is difficult, but now that they are gone, I'm looking forward to their replacements. It wasn't a matching set, anyway. I will probably venture out some tomorrow after I see my doctors.

PART
II

Now What?

CLOSE ENCOUNTERS OF THE HER2 KIND

August 15, 2014

Today was a big day! Follow-up appointments with both of my surgeons. First, I saw Dr. B., my plastic surgeon. She said that everything looked good, just as it should. I got the drains out and, the best part, had the tight ace bandage removed. Feels so good to be out of that! Now I'm in a cotton sports bra that is a bit tight to help keep the swelling down. There are just two little spots where the drains were to clean and watch for a few days until they seal up. YAY, I CAN TAKE A SHOWER! The sponge baths worked, but a shower is going to be amazing! I see her again in a week to start the saline injections.

Surprisingly, I didn't have much reaction to seeing my

chest. It was strange but didn't elicit any deep emotions. I think I had already adjusted to seeing my flat self in the bandage. There is still a lot going on in the front. There are the doctor's purple markings, some orange coloring from the prep liquid used, a few stitches, some tape over the incisions, and a little yellow bruising. I was told there will be some swelling and bruising in the coming days. I think it will be a while before I can see how it truly looks. I feel okay with it, though. It's a relief to have the defective parts removed.

Next, it was on to my general surgeon's office, Dr. W. He is very concerned that his patients are comfortable with all of their care. He told me that he was impressed at how I've just flown through all of this with a smile on my face. He said he liked me and that quality. Of course, a little later I shed a few tears and he was worried that he upset me. It's so important to like your doctors and have confidence in them. I have a great team!

This appointment was about the pathology report and

what's next. The cancer has been removed; I am CURRENTLY CANCER FREE! The devil is in the details, though. I thought it would be easy peasy, take it out and go on but there is much to be determined by the complete pathology report. They can see from the margins that all of the tumor has been removed. Details of the complete testing show that it was an aggressive tumor, Grade 3, that was heading into the lymph system but didn't make it to the nodes. There were also additional pre-cancerous cells in other areas. The translation here is that I made the right decision and timing was crucial. Had it not been found this early, it would have grown and gotten into my lymph nodes. Had I opted for a lumpectomy to just remove the tumor instead of mastectomy to remove all the tissue, there would have been other cancers show up.

Now, the devilish details. The tumor was positive for both estrogen and progesterone receptors. This means that the cancer I had responds to the female hormones. That is what makes it grow and how it can be treated with hormone therapy drugs. The other important thing is if it is HER2 positive. Breast cancers with extra HER2 receptors tend to be more aggressive. The tumor was positive for this in one test and neither positive nor negative in another. That is unusual and doesn't have a clear-cut answer for treatment. If it is Her2 positive, a specific drug is suggested. The good thing about this treatment, Herceptin, is that it goes directly to those certain cancer cells and sets them up for destruction by the immune system.

You probably wonder why it matters since the cancer is gone and didn't spread. The reality is that there's no way to know if any of the cells got into the bloodstream and are waiting to pop up somewhere else. Having the details will determine the best way to treat and eradicate any errant cells as a precaution. I am all about going after anything that might have escaped. I am not that thrilled about the idea of any kind of chemo, though. As much as my hair frustrates me, I don't want to lose it. The thought of losing my eyelashes also really bothers me. It's just hair and I guess that's kind of vain, but it is part of my identity. First no boobs, then no hair. I guess that by the time I would start this, I would have my chest back or mostly. If the boob job is good enough maybe it will detract from my bald head. I always try to find the silver lining, so I'm thinking maybe it will grow back curly. I'm a little afraid that it's going to come back grayer. Not the end of the world, I just want to live, with hair or without, straight or curly, black, or gray. If that's what it comes to, I will rock some awesome hats and/or wigs; let my honey explore some fantasies. The big takeaway for the day is BREAST CANCER DEFEATED! ASS HAS BEEN KICKED!! NEXT...

The day started well. After a week of feeling like I had a large tourniquet wrapped around my upper body, there was instant relief when it was removed. I was happy to know that things were healing well and there were no signs of any post-surgical issues. At the time, equally important was the thought of getting a shower.

Both my mom and husband joined me for the surgeon's appointment. I was glad for the support when I received unexpected news about the cancer and suggested follow-up treatment.

The doctor started the appointment by commenting on how he loved my good attitude and cheerfulness and how I breezed right through the surgery; then he laid the good news on me about having removed all of the cancer. I had no qualms about having a complete mastectomy; that had always been my plan. Knowing that the tumor had "fingers" that were reaching out toward the lymph nodes confirmed that my surgical decision was the correct one. Verification of complete removal made me a survivor; the cancer was gone.

After confirmation of my cancer-free status, doc hit me with the news that the cancer was Grade 3 out of 3, for aggressiveness and, most likely, triple positive. I anticipated that it would be hormone-positive, that's what the other cases in my family had been, but I didn't know anything about the Her2 protein or what that meant for treatment. I was expecting to just go on about my business, but things became more complicated with the introduction of that possibility.

After laying out the cancerous details and treatment suggestions, the doctor left the room for a few minutes. I sat there under the heavy weight of his words working to process what he had just said. After a little silence, I looked from my husband to my mom and felt the tears start to come. Emotion welled up and I couldn't stop it. Never in my wildest imagination did I expect to face chemo. When Dr. W. came back into the room and saw that I had been crying, he felt bad thinking that he had upset me. I told him it was alright; the talk of chemo just took me by surprise.

With me having no experience with or thoughts on a specific oncologist, Dr. W. told me of the one he intended to refer me to. That conversation included a very important sentiment. Doc said that if I didn't like who he sent me to, then he would find me a different doctor, and if I didn't like the next one, we would look into another until I found the oncologist that was right for me. That is a crucial idea that I appreciated and have passed along to other newly diagnosed friends who I have talked with. It is so important that you like and trust all your doctors since your team truly has your life in their hands. That is a point that I cannot stress enough.

I left that appointment with much to consider and a big decision in treatment to be made. My doctor was recommending chemo and that was a shocker. I had some thinking, praying, and research to do.

August 16, 2014

Wow, a shower! What an amazing luxury! After not having running water on my body for a week and a half, that was the best feeling ever. Don't get me wrong, I was clean, washed every day, but a washcloth cleaning doesn't compare to a nice hot shower. I stood there with the water pouring on me for what seemed like forever. Next, it was time for the big unveiling to my husband. He couldn't be at my first appointment yesterday, so he hadn't yet seen the new landscape of my chest. It is starting to bruise, so that adds color and confusion to what is going on. I couldn't quite get a read on him, so I'm not sure just how freaked out he was. I feel like he's trying hard to be okay with everything. Maybe he is, I won't know for sure because he's not going to let me know if it bothers him. These are the times when I get emotional, when Eric is involved. I feel like this isn't fair to him. We are newlyweds. We're supposed to be enjoying our new lives together, not sleeping separately so that I can be propped up with pillows and ice bags that he has become faithful in filling. He has slid into the caretaker role effortlessly and he is an amazing blessing. I just want to get back to husband and wife, not patient and caregiver.

The one good takeaway today came after the shower when I was standing there looking at my whole self in the full-length mirror. What I realized is that the remainder of this almost 45-year-old, in three days, body is holding up pretty well. I'm not at all upset with the way everything else is looking. When the rest of me gets fixed up, watch out!

August 19, 2014 – IT'S MY BIRTHDAY!

This one moves me to the next age demographic. That's okay, at least I'm still here! I started my day a little down about "celebrating" in this state, but that has changed. A dear friend came and had lunch with me, another is on the way over, I got a delivery from work that made me smile and the outpouring of well-wishes and virtual love overwhelms me! Thank you all for making my day so special!

That was not the way that I had expected to spend my 45th birthday, but it turned out to be a great day. I was feeling good and enjoyed time with friends and family. I was also delivered a poster from my coworkers. It was filled with sweet birthday wishes that made me feel missed. I appreciate my work family. It was a wonderful surprise delivery that came in addition to a multi-tiered snack box that provided goodies for quite a while.

Things like cards, meal deliveries and shared meals, snacks, and a fun ice cream delivery from a friend one day, made the time recovering easier. Gestures like that can seem simple to the person making them but mean the world to the recipient. I already knew that I was blessed with amazingly special people in my life, but my experiences throughout this journey have magnified that point.

LIVING ON THE EDGE

August 30, 2014 (5:54 pm)

Apart from my birthday a week and a half ago, I haven't posted anything. I figure it is time to catch up. The reason that I went "radio silent" was due to some of your comments on my page. So many of you have remarked about how brave and inspirational that I am. Honestly, for the past couple of weeks, I haven't felt brave or inspirational. This whole thing has thrown me for a loop. I wasn't prepared for the emotional twists and turns of this ride I've been on.

I kind of coasted through that first week after surgery. I was feeling good, determined, strong, ready to press on and move forward. Then, the weekend after my follow-up surgical visits, I hit a wall. In retrospect, I realize that part of the reason I was feeling so good early on and had that outlook was that I was continually medicated with a very good pain reliever. I hit my wall when I stopped taking the meds regularly. That, combined with the news from my surgeon about further treatment and a physical situation, took me to the brink.

I already posted about the surgical follow-ups. The weekend following that brought a new enemy and pain like I have not experienced probably since childbirth. Constipation! Ugh! That inflamed the dreaded hemorrhoids, a gift from my first pregnancy. Seriously!?! I had just gone through major surgery with very little pain, and I was brought to my knees by my bowels being uncooperative. Horrible pain! No one told me that pain meds could do that until after the fact. I knew the first BM after surgery was important and I kind of celebrated when it happened, but it wasn't all that was needed. I spent that weekend, crying, pleading, doing everything that I could to find relief and to move things along. Fiber, laxatives, sitting in hot baths, Witch Hazel, and Preparation H. Two days of absolute hell followed by several days of a lighter version of hell, and then things gradually getting better. That is when I stopped taking the pain meds and when I went over the edge.

It was unexpected and awful! That got me down, then I started thinking about the possible treatments to follow and the pain in my chest from the expanders and I just kept going down. Crying, a lot, for no reason but frustration with the whole situation. I was not even two weeks in and was totally over all of it. I feel bad for my patient, loving husband. There are still times that he looks at me and I cry and can't always explain why. I just want to feel normal again. I want to be able to lay down in my bed without being propped up with pillows and roll on my side. I want to snuggle up with my honey, to plop down on the couch in any fashion, to lift anything that I need to, to be able to breathe fully and not shallow and to not have this pain in my chest. Every move I make is deliberate. A jolt in the car, a sneeze or cough, even a laugh, moves things in my chest and causes more pain, even if just for a moment. I shouldn't complain, I chose this. It's necessary to regain a close to natural-looking chest in the future but it's genuinely uncomfortable.

These heavy plastic bags don't belong behind my chest muscle and my body is complaining. It feels much like this: take a flat piece of wood and strap it across your chest, then tighten it as much as possible and leave it there. It is hard to breathe and every time I move, I feel this pressing on my chest. I can feel with my hands the sides of the bags under my arms. I need to get sat into just the right position to take some of the pressure off so that I can almost be comfortable.

As I had started to make peace with my new hardware and be able to get up and out and around, I went for the first injections to start the filling process. That made things worse. Looks like I will get to live with these until the first of the year. Hopefully, as things stretch and I get more used to it, the discomfort won't be so bad. Okay, whining over that done. Next, where do I go from here?

I saw my oncologist last week and that visit sent me down another path. Because of the pathology of my disease, I will be undergoing four months of chemo, a year of Herceptin infusions, and five years of Tamoxifen in pill form. I truly didn't expect chemo. My cancer was Stage 1, clear margins, no node involvement, all removed with surgery, seemed like a simple road. I went into this a little blind to the possibilities. I always thought that when it was my turn to head down this path that it would be as simple as removing it and following it with five years of a drug for hormone receptive cancer. Nope, not so easy.

With the cancer being Grade 3 and assuming it is Her2 positive, as well as double hormone-positive, it is more threatening. The good news is that the protocol to directly treat triple-positive cancers is effective in shutting them down and killing off the cells. An overabundance of HER2 protein receptors causes the cancer cells to grow and divide more rapidly. The fear is in the possibility of secondary cancers down the road due to any of those cells that may have escaped into my bloodstream. With Stage 1, clear margins, no node involvement, and early detection, the likelihood is slim that there is any in my blood, but the possibility exists. If there is even the smallest chance that any has escaped, I want to take it out.

I have been reading about the chemo drugs that I will be taking and the Herceptin that will follow for a year and the Tamoxifen that I will take for five years after that. They all have their own special kind of risks; some of them are serious and possibly not reversible. The oncologist truly believes that the benefits outweigh the risks. I will trust that he knows what he's doing. I'm going to be quite upset, though, if I don't have any other cancer cells to kill and I end up with liver problems, heart failure, lung issues, leukemia, or cervical cancer from one of the drugs that I'm going to take. Those are some of the worst possibilities. They are rare but do happen. I am praying that the worst side effect that I have is baldness.

One of the big disappointments in all of this is having to cancel our cruise in October. It was to be the honeymoon that we didn't have and a celebration of our first anniversary. It will be postponed and hopefully, we will be able to go in the spring when most of this is over and I have begun to move forward. I'm still trying to dig out of this hole that I've fallen into. Working to find my fight again. I will get back there, I have to, I don't want to let you all down. I have had such overwhelming support that I can't wallow in this, I must get back up and face this head-on. I can't even express how much it means to have all of you behind me. The constant encouragement helps me to keep looking forward.

This post doesn't need much extra explanation, it lays it out rather well. Multiple situations started me spiraling down and I couldn't post without being negative and showing how scared and vulnerable I was feeling. I was afraid that I wasn't going to get back up to feeling good. Like a child who has done something wrong or is embarrassed and avoids their parents, I was hiding from my readers. I wanted to be positive and encouraging and strong. I felt like I had to be some kind of superhero but realized that I'm only human and that comes with challenges. In retrospect, it is better to expose that side of humanity. Doing so actually shows the strength and courage that I thought I was missing.

The comments on my posts and interactions with everyone helped keep me going and push me forward. When putting this book together, I decided not to include any of the comments that go with the posts. I felt it would be too hard to choose which ones to keep and which to leave out; I didn't want to exclude anyone, and I had the length of the book to consider. There was one comment on this post, however, that I was compelled to incorporate. It is well written and makes a strong point about the notion of bravery.

"I haven't had a chance to reply before now, so I apologize for dragging this up, but I thought I had something to add. People sometimes have a strange conception of 'bravery'. Maybe it comes from watching too many Sylvester Stallone movies; I'm not sure. Anyway, some people seem to think that 'bravery' means not being afraid or not letting anything bother you. That's silly. I have no fear of brushing my teeth, so it's not even slightly brave for me to do it. In a life-or-death situation – and make no mistake, that's what you've been in – being unafraid, or unflappable, or any of those things, is not being brave, it's being ignorant, or stupid, or reckless. I do not get the impression that you are any of those things.

Being brave is, quite simply, being afraid – being terrified – and doing what you need to do anyway. Being brave is Captain Sullenberger, who landed that plane in the Hudson River, and who said it was "the worst sickening, pit-of-your-stomach, falling-through-the-floor feeling that I had ever experienced." Being brave is Nelson Mandela, who said, 'The brave man is not he who does not feel afraid, but he who conquers that fear."

Everybody has bad days. You can't expect to avoid them, but you can face them, deal with them, and move past them. Soon, they'll be coming less often. No, you don't have to try to be an inspiration to anybody, but you know what? You are, anyway. Your bravery comes through in every word, even – especially – in a post like this.

Fight the good fight. You're winning." – Patrick

Thank you, Patrick, for such wise words.

(8:18 pm)

I forgot this in my previous post. When we were sitting in the oncology office waiting for the doctor, I noticed the one magazine in the wall rack and found it very telling. The title of the magazine was something like, "All About Slots". Not sure that was it, but it was about playing slots and gambling. Therein lies the rub; the whole thing with the chemo and follow-up is a gamble.

You either don't do treatment and lay odds that there's nothing more to take care of or you do treatment without knowing if there is anything there needing it. Also, you are betting that you are getting the right treatment and it won't make you sick in a different way. It's all a bit of a crapshoot!

I found it funny that was the one magazine in there. Don't get me wrong, I am more than grateful that these options are available. Probably more times than not they are lifesavers or at least extenders; it just struck me as funny.

CH CH CH CH CHOICES

September 1, 2014

I am struggling with the chemo decision. It seems extreme with my Stage 1, no node situation. My mom had breast cancer twice, once each breast, and each time had lumpectomy and radiation. She also did not complete a regimen of Tamoxifen. She has been more than 23 years out from the first occurrence and 18 from the second with no further issues. I don't know the Her2 status of her cancer; I'm not sure if they even tested for that back when she was diagnosed. I am reading a lot and now chemo seems to be the preferred protocol for Her2 positive breast cancer.

I want to have as many years as possible left on this

planet, so I need to do the right thing to try and ensure I don't face this again. It truly is such a gamble. So hard to know what is going to be right. If I do it, I'm filling my healthy body with poison and risking other issues. If I don't and this cancer travels and grows somewhere else, it will be more of a problem. My family history is brutal, and I lost my grandmother and an aunt to untreated breast cancer. I know that, when given a chance, it will set up in other places and it wouldn't take long to spread. It's an incredibly difficult decision to make. I would like to squeeze about another 40 years out of this body. I want to do what is best, I'm just unsure of what that is.

Her2 stands for Human Epidermal Growth Factor Receptor 2. These proteins are found on all breast cells and promote their health and growth. Cancerous cells with higher-than-normal levels of Her2 protein receptors, are considered Her2 positive (Her2+) and tend to grow and divide quicker, making the cancer more aggressive. Cancerous breast tumors are now routinely tested for Her2 levels. With mine showing higher levels in one test but inconclusive in another, the grey area it fell into made deciding on treatment less clear cut.

Because of the Her2 test results, Dr. W. suggested treating my cancer as triple positive. He assured me that in the case of breast cancer, being positive is a good thing because of the specific and effective treatments. Herceptin is an antibody that attaches itself to the Her2 receptors and helps to slow down cell growth and may encourage the immune system to rid the body of the cancerous cells. Herceptin is given as an infusion for a year and doesn't carry the possibility of most of the ugly side effects of chemo. The downside, though, is that it is said to work best when paired with chemotherapy to get it started.

The decision to go the route of chemo or not was huge; there was much to consider. How would it affect me? I didn't want to get sick. I didn't want to lose my hair. The possibility of the chemo causing other health complications or bringing on a different cancer worried me. Choosing not to do it, though, would either mean not having the Herceptin for the Her2 issue or having Herceptin, but it not being as effective. I had come to know that a year of Herceptin treatment was the best means to shut down the Her2 protein-loaded cells, should any remain. That factor made my decision. Pairing chemo with Herceptin would create the lowest probability for breast cancer recurrence or the occurrence of future related cancers. There wasn't much question, it's what I needed to do.

September 3, 2014

Woohoo! Today I was able to lift and straighten my arms enough to completely shave under them. Celebrating a minor victory. Funny the small things you can appreciate.

September 4, 2014 (11:04am)

Time to get cut on again. Port placement today. More foreign objects inside my chest.

(4:00 pm)

Back home, the port is in place. Ready for next week. I have been thinking about something a lot through all of this and again today. We are blessed with amazing health care here. I am immensely thankful to be dealing with this in the U.S. and my hometown. All the facilities are top-notch and the staff that I have dealt with have been wonderful. Being put at ease by well-trained and compassionate people makes things so much better. Every nurse, tech, and doctor that I have seen has shown a great bedside manner, explained everything in detail, and treated me with the utmost respect. They have shown compassion and humor and have made otherwise scary situations easier to deal with. I know that costs are out of control and insurance is a mess and sometimes hard to deal with, but the care and human side of it is a blessing. Just a little food for thought.

LESSONS AFOOT

September 6, 2014

What a beautifully crisp day today. My kind of weather! A glimpse of fall to come. So nice to get out for a walk with my handsome husband. A little cruise around our subdivision. Normally I can cover our whole side at a pretty good pace and be ready to go further. Today, I had to cut it short; was getting a little dizzy and a bit hard to breathe. I blame the expanders for the breathing and lack of activity for the dizziness. Looking for good weather this week to get out and walk more.

Have you ever watched a grown woman struggle to tie her shoes? That's what my husband got to do before our walk. So frustrating not being able to easily do some of the simplest things these days. The addition of this port has added just enough tightness and awkwardness to my left side that I couldn't bend enough or pull hard enough to adequately lace up my shoes. It's been a long time since I've had to ask to have my shoes tied.

These little things are what cause me the most frustration, partly because I'm a Leo and just a little bit of a control freak, but mostly because I have always been so independent. Being the only child of a single, working mom, I learned to do for myself early on. In addition, being the main parent to two boys, I relied on myself to take care of things. These days I am slow-moving and awkward. I can't simply jump up out of a chair or slide in and out of the car. When I reach for something, I have to maneuver my entire body to get my arm where it needs to go. Looking forward to getting back to the status quo.

This is teaching me to be more thoughtful of others. I have realized that we never know what someone else is dealing with. I need to have more patience. When I am behind someone in the supermarket who is moving slow or in my way, I will give them the time that they need. I won't know what their situation is, but it might be something like mine. As it is right now, I could be that person slowing you down; not doing it on purpose, but because that's how I'm moving right now. Then again, some people are just inconsiderate and get in your way for no good reason other than that they don't care. Most times you won't know which is the case but what's a few extra seconds in the grand scheme of things? Someday it might be you who needs those additional seconds. Everyone has their own fight, but ultimately, we're in this life together and should have more patience with those around us.

Journeys such as this have many teachable moments. Realizing my need for assistance and extra time to accomplish the smallest things, made me hyper-aware of that in others. As I mentioned, I am a Leo, and, although I don't much buy into astrology, some of the personality traits associated with the zodiac signs line up well.

The independence attributed to Leos is on point. Needing help to tie my shoes was a humbling and eye-opening experience. Since then, I have attempted to be more patient and compassionate with others and consider what could be going on in their lives that might affect what they are doing. That hasn't quite transferred to driving, however, I still have a bit of road rage. People who don't go when the light turns green or who cut others off or haven't figured out how to use the magical device that makes your lights flicker and is known as a turn signal can send my blood boiling. Sorry, went a little off track. Still working to transfer patience to driving. My point is, we all need to be more thoughtful of others. That could come back to you in a time that you need it most.

September 7, 2014

Practical things I have learned so far in this adventure:

- Getting up from chairs and out of bed without using your arms helps to strengthen your core. It is also quite funny and provides comic relief for those around you while it takes about three times as long as it normally would.

- Bags of frozen peas do work better than ice bags. Your drinks won't suffer from depleted ice reserves, and they can be turned into a tasty side dish for dinner in a pinch. This was a greatly appreciated tip from my plastic surgeon.

- Cornstarch works wonders to soothe chafed underarms. The combination of swelling, not shaving, and being unable to move your arms too far off, causes distressing chafing. I mentioned this issue to a new friend who is a fellow survivor and was in the midst of reconstruction and she told me of this marvel. It was funny when Eric walked into the bathroom to find a large container of cornstarch.

He looked at me and asked if I was making cookies in there. Nope, just powdering my pits!

- Feminine pads work well as substitutes for gauze to cover incisions. This was a handy hint passed along from my plastic surgeon's nurse. They are larger, softer, and don't stick to wounds. Get the cheaper ones without wings. After all, you don't need the aeronautical-add-ons since you won't be flying anytime soon. Bonus, if you expose the sticky on the back and cover it with cotton balls when you put these in your bra, it provides a nice A cup situation. Just like being a teenager again.

In summary, at any given time, you can find me with feminine pads either taped to my chest or padding my bra while I nuzzle frozen peas under arms with pits coated in your basic sauce thickener. Just another day in the breast cancer battle.

September 8, 2014

Here are a couple of additional things that were left off my practical lessons list yesterday:

- Going without makeup and simplifying your hairstyle will not kill you or overly frighten anyone else. In the last month, I have not put base makeup on at all, I have worn blush three times and have used my curling iron only once. I may be making assumptions in thinking that I'm still presentable, but I haven't seen anyone staring and pointing and no children have run from me screaming. I am enjoying this newfound freedom from routine. Mascara and lip color are still a daily must, but I have become comfortable with an otherwise fresh face. Because of my slower pace and continuing to deal with incision maintenance, it still takes me almost the same amount of time to get ready as before, though.

- Having monkey toes is a great asset when recovering from surgery. I am blessed with the ability to pick up a myriad of items with both of my piggies who went to market as well as the two who stayed home. Not having to bend down to retrieve things has been a great help these past weeks. I have been perfecting this skill since childhood. It was first brought to my attention by my maternal grandmother who used her toes to pinch. Her pinching toes were legendary. Nights with her would include running from those vicious toes, which are some of the fondest memories of my grandma. Despite years of practice, I never quite perfected effective pinching, but I can pick up almost anything.

That post included a shout-out to my maternal grandma, Clarice a/k/a Grandma Stephens. I spent a lot of time growing up with both of my grandmas and miss each of them dearly. Grandma Stephens instilled in me a love of the St. Louis Cardinals and the ability to utilize my toes for more than walking. She is the reason that my breast cancer ribbon tattoo has a halo. When her cancer was diagnosed, it had already spread to her bones and organs, but the originating cancer was found to be breast. It was thought that she may have had a breast lump for years that was never investigated. That oversight likely caused us to be cheated of extra time with her. Never ignore breast changes or a lump, no matter how small or seemingly insignificant. That could rob your family of additional years of love to share. Signs that may be overlooked include breast pain, skin dimpling, and nipple discharge, either bloody or oily. Investigate anything that doesn't seem right.

LET'S GET READY TO RUMBLE

September 9, 2014 (11:55 am)

Goodbye long hair! Off to get my pre-chemo cut. This is the one time that it doesn't matter how it turns out because I'll probably be losing it in the next two weeks anyway. Kind of excited for a new look.

(2:00 pm)

I love my new cut! It got the thumbs up from my honey. Going from long hair to an above-the-shoulder bob took off about six inches or so.

(4:00 pm)

I have made peace with the treatment that I am heading for. Never in my craziest dreams did I expect to be facing chemo. I was a little too naive about the whole situation. I watched my mom face breast cancer twice with limited treatment. She is a couple decades past her second time with no further issues. I thought that when my time came, I would remove it and go on. I knew I would opt for a double mastectomy, just to be safe, and I expected to do five years on Tamoxifen for the hormonal aspect, but I figured that would be it. Having the doctor tell me that my cancer was aggressive, and I needed to do chemotherapy followed by another eight months of an infusion drug floored me.

I greatly struggled with the idea of chemo. It's poison and will attack and kill healthy cells in my body. The possible side effects are not enjoyable, and some are downright scary. When it's all said and done, though, the purpose is to wipe out any of the aggressive cancer cells that may have gotten into my bloodstream and I'm all about that. If I can reduce my chances of going head-to-head with this again in any form to 10% or lower, I will do what it takes. Maybe I would be just fine not doing the chemo, but why risk it? Now is the time to wipe out any remnants. I have done much reading about the drugs I'll be taking on cancer sites and blogs and have explored stories of women with the same diagnosis and treatment. I feel good about moving forward with this. I'm young(ish) and healthy and ready to meet this full-on. I'm not going in blindly. I'm preparing for some of the more common side effects with nutrition and things that might help prevent them, but I'm choosing to think positively and try not to expect them. My friend told me about going with her grandmother for her chemo treatments and how this one woman would come in all done up with big hair and heels and would do her nails. It was just another item on her to-do list; it was not going to keep her down. My friend said, "Be that lady." I'm going to be that lady!

September 10, 2014 (11:01 am)

Waiting at the plastic surgeon for my second saline fill. She uses what she calls her stud finder to locate the metal part of the expander where she will inject. She said that her younger patients always ask if she can find them a stud with that. The answer is NO. The fill itself doesn't much hurt, just a couple of quick needle sticks. After, though, the chest pressure will get tighter, and it will hurt for the rest of the day. That is what happened the first time, maybe it will be better today. I am anticipating some pain meds in my future. I am very thankful to have the option of reconstruction and to be a patient of one of the best around. That makes the discomfort worth it.

(11:38 am)

Bummer! Had to put the fill off for another week. The incision on the left is closing very slowly. There is a good two-inch area that is not yet healed. I have been applying a prescribed cream for the past week and a half and it has gotten better, but not good enough. I asked if it was going to be okay and was told yes, but I'm "not breaking any healing records". Doc cut on it to remove some of the tissue and said she didn't want to fill and increase the pressure from the inside, wanted a little more healing time. Thanks to the bit of cutting and cleaning that she did, I didn't get the fill, but still got the pain. Bump in the road to building better boobs. Not a big deal, more of a disappointment to make a trip for nothing. I'm going to have these expanders until the first of the year since I can't complete reconstruction until chemo is concluded. There is plenty of time to fill. I'll reach my preferred size way before I'm able to have them switched out.

THAT GIRL IS (filled with) POISON

September 12, 2014 (7:58am)

Chemo #1

Big day! Heading in for my first chemo treatment. One of six. Ready to knock these out! Let's do this!

My sweet husband surprised me on that epic morning by wearing a new shirt that said, "I WEAR PINK FOR MY WIFE". He also presented me with a special necklace made of a rhinestone encrusted, pink ribbon adorned dog tag engraved with a Bible verse speaking of strength.

(9:52 am)

Here we go! Thank you for all the love and support!

(12:20 pm)

I am set up in my own little "pod" in the new cancer

center. It's a nice area where I will be spending every third Friday until the end of the year. Lots of windows, a comfy chair, my own TV, and a friendly staff constantly checking on my comfort. I also have an array of beverages and cookies at my disposal. I'm covered with warmed blankets and can have all the pillows that I desire. Again, I say, I am extremely grateful for the wonderful medical care that I am receiving.

Each treatment is about a six-to-six-and-a-half-hour event. It starts with a doctor visit, then labs, and then I find a place to park myself and get settled in. Once I'm nice and cozy, chair-side service begins. The appetizer combo in this liquid banquet consists of an injection of something strong for nausea and a steroid infusion. The steroid should help to keep down the inflammation and make things as smooth as possible. After those two are completed, there is a flush for half an hour to cleanse the palate and then the fun begins. The main course is a lovely bag of Taxotere in a light reduction, served for an hour. This is the heavy hitter in the mix. It will be the one that takes my hair. That will be followed by a heaping bowl of Carboplatin for an hour with a delicious hour and a half of Herceptin for dessert. I'm sure this feast will leave me over-filled and ready for a nap. A cancer patient's Thanksgiving, for which I am giving many thanks.

(12:52 pm)

Two courses down, dessert has been served. I got this!

(3:58 pm)

Thought I would share what I have packed in my chemo bag. When I was getting it together last night, it felt like I was preparing for a trip. In a sense, I guess I was.

I brought a tote with my Kindle and some paper and cards I need to work on. I haven't touched any of those.

In a bright, happy little bag, that I will keep for each time, I have the following:

- a compact - always like to have a little mirror handy so I can check that I don't have anything in my teeth or hanging from my nose

- a bright pink lipstick - well, yeah!
- nail clippers and a file - have been needing to get my nails under control

- small package of tissues - I have read that runny eyes and nose can be a side effect and in case of possible, aforementioned, nose danglers

- hand sanitizer - I am now a germ-free zone

- gum and hard mint candy - to aid in saliva flow to head off dry mouth and possible mouth sores

- tube of Vaseline - to keep lips moist, got this during my hospital stay after surgery, I'm guessing it's a very expensive tube of lip lube

- a couple of granola bars - you know what those are for

- Fannie May Mint Cookie dark chocolate candy bar - because this is the most wonderful treat on the planet, and I figure this deserves just a little treat.

Today, I also brought some grapes and a 32oz bottle of water with lemon, cucumber, and mint. Topped it all off with my charming wit and sparkling personality. Boom!

(4:03 pm)

Amen! Today's mission accomplished! One down, five to go. I am one-sixth of the way through my chemo plan. With the steroid, three bags of drugs, and saline flushes between each, I have had eight bags of fluid today. Does anyone who knows me want to guess how many times I have peed? I am now a pro at unhooking the charger on the IV stand and wheeling my friend along for potty breaks.

(4:31 pm)

I feel like a supervillain with poison surging through my veins! Muahahaha (maniacal laugh)! Just call me Poison Ivy! Really, though, I'm tired and feeling a tiny bit queasy. I could have slept some at treatment, but don't want videos of my snoring going viral. Ready to put on PJs and hug the couch for the night.

(7:17 pm)

Tonight's dinner is brought to you by the letter "S", for small portions, safe and soothing:

- Scrambled eggs - protein, check!
- Applesauce - fruit, check!

- Ginger Ale - tummy calmer, check!

- Tapioca pudding - comfort, check!

Waiting to see if it all stays down where I put it...

- curiosity, check!

September 13, 2014

Time for an update on chemo night number one. Last night was not too bad. I was tired and a little nauseous. I ate light, took the anti-nausea meds, and hit the couch around 7:30. I woke up to my cat standing on my chest, staring at me with her one big green eye and yapping at me viciously about wanting to be fed. This is the norm for her, and it usually takes place around 2:30 in the morning. I didn't remember even getting close to falling asleep and figured that it was the middle of the night. I was a bit disoriented and was coming around when Eric walked into the room. He was all bright-eyed with Kindle in hand, asking me what I needed. I was confused, he was way too chipper for it to be so late. I looked at the time and it was only 9:30. He said I had been asleep for an hour and a half. It is more like I was out cold for an hour and a half. Odd feeling!

At that point, I had another hour and a half before I could take any more anti-nausea medicine and I felt like I needed it. Had that feeling at the bottom of my throat that I might not be able to hold back what was wanting to come up for a visit. My mouth was dry. I had a little water and a peppermint and decided to get ready for bed. I fed my cat, because, she was right, it was time for her bedtime feeding and I wanted her to stop yelling at me. She is funny, she "talks" a lot and very emphatically. While she was happily scarfing down an obnoxious pile of meat chunks in gravy, I went to take care of myself.

I brushed my teeth with one of the six new, soft toothbrushes that I had stocked up on. To minimize germs here, I will rotate these out at least every two weeks and keep the current one in a plastic travel case. On a side note, you can run your travel toothbrush case through the dishwasher; just set each end over one of the glass spindles on the top shelf. Handy hint from Lisa.

Brushed with Biotene toothpaste for dry mouth and sensitive situations. Brushing was followed by a rinse with Biotene mouthwash. It is moisturizing to help prevent dry mouth, non-irritating, and alcohol-free. I want very much to prevent mouth sores, if possible. I dried off with my personal hand towel that I have set up in the master bath, which will be the only one that I use from now on, if possible, the towel and the bathroom.

I am not typically a germaphobe. I have been that mom that figures that a little bit of dirt and sticky things on hands won't hurt but will help build immunity. Depending on where we are, I don't have a problem with the "five-second rule". I keep my house clean but don't follow people around with a cloud of Lysol or take a Clorox wipe to every door handle and light switch daily. Well, that has changed. I need to be in as germ-free an environment as possible when my white blood count drops. There is a large bottle of hand sanitizer by the front door, and I have told the boys they need to wash their hands more than ever before. You have to remind boys of that, it doesn't seem to come naturally.

Unfortunately, I have a child who has picked up a cold. I am pushing vitamin C and juice at him. I heard my stepson sneeze this morning and my cat even sneezed right on me. I may have to put myself in a bubble. Now, returning from my little tangent. I finished my bedtime routine by cleaning and redressing my incisions. As soon as I was able to take another pill, I went off to bed with a glass of water and some Chapstick and actually got some good sleep.

September 13 – contd.
Day 2

I woke up this morning feeling a little nauseous with a dry mouth. Laid around and snuggled with my husband and cat for a bit then slowly worked my way to upright. I opted for a protein shake for breakfast with some strawberries and a banana. I used that to wash down my anti-nausea pill, which is Zofran and supposed to be very effective, a daily multi-vitamin, vitamin C, and a Colace.

Colace is a stool softener that you can take daily. It was suggested to me by a nurse who I was telling about my constipation horror story. I don't want to go there again and one of the side effects of the chemo and the Zofran is constipation.

My activity has been minimal today. Not feeling great. I have a bit of a headache, as well. It's not awful, I know it could be worse. The nausea reminds me of the morning sickness I had with both pregnancies. Morning sickness is a misnomer, it lasted all day. Just a total yuck feeling that wouldn't go away. I am only making a comparison and not suggesting that this is morning sickness, thankfully! In this stage of my life, the idea of going back to bottles and diapers and walking the floor with a crying baby, makes me want to hide in a padded room. I love babies and look forward to grandchildren in the future, but my personal baby days are over. I know for certain this is chemo nausea because, not only did I have a pregnancy test before the surgery to implant my port, but also because it would be another immaculate conception at this point. The change in physical intimacy is a whole other discussion.

Had a small lunch of an egg on whole-wheat toast, 3 pretzels, and a glass of milk with a dose of MiraLAX. As I said, I want to make sure things will flow freely. I am trying to be very thoughtful of my nutrition during this time but, right now, focusing more on things that will give me what I need and are less likely to revisit later. I am currently holding down my end of the couch and watching Netflix with Jake and the cat, who was "helping" me to write this earlier by lying on my lap in front of the computer.

September 14, 2014

Day 3

THIS SUCKS!! No other way to put it. Constant nausea and headache. I'm so tired that I just fall asleep without seeing it coming. I randomly woke up without even realizing I was asleep. Weird! I really wanted to go to church this morning. I headed to the shower at 8:30 am and finally made it there at 12:30. I couldn't get past the bed. Hoping this starts to pass soon. I can't imagine trying to function like this for too long. I need to get back to work and this won't cut it. I can tell that I am going to have to take full advantage of the times that I feel good. My fighting spirit is still here, but it's especially tired!

September 15, 2014

Day 4

Today was not as completely awful as yesterday. The nausea is somewhat under control. It is taking two meds to keep it that way. Headache has subsided, too. My face has started breaking out and my nose is runny. Feel like I'm getting something in the back of my throat but hoping that's just from the sinus drainage running that way. Still extremely tired and weak. I spent most of the day sleeping to avoid it all.

Got a shot today, Neulasta, to help with my white blood count. It is supposed to work on the bone marrow and stimulate the production of white blood cells. This should help things bounce back quicker. Hoping tomorrow is better and that I will start climbing back.

September 16
Day 5

Today things are getting better. I continue to be weak and tired, but the rest is settling down. The tissue expanders in my chest are bothering me more than anything. They seem so much tighter and are truly uncomfortable. I guess that's going to be the back and forth throughout this. My cat has decided that she needs to nuzzle right at my neck now. She gets in there then puts her "arm" around my neck. I hope she's hugging me and not trying to choke me out. The thing is, with cats, you just never know.

September 17, 2014
Day 6

I am finally seeing the light again. Feeling close to human. Still weak and tiring very easily. That part is annoying me. I did get out to enjoy the beautiful fall-like weather today and took a walk. I had to be covered from head to toe because of being photosensitive, but it was cool enough that it was warranted. Went once around the block. I was able to tie my shoes alone; the last time I couldn't.

Currently, I'm dealing with just a few side effects. I'm very fatigued. I have a bad taste in my mouth that affects most of what I eat. Water doesn't even taste good, and it usually doesn't have much of a taste. Smells are starting to bother me, too. My skin is breaking out badly. I don't have a rash on my face, but there's a bit of one further down. I will just say that there is a product in the baby aisle called "butt paste", which is extremely soothing. This is reality. I'm thankful that, so far, nausea has subsided.

I'm not doing cartwheels yet, because some things don't kick in until seven to ten days after treatment. I'm going to think positive and hope the worst is over. I basically slept for four days to get through it. I know my family is tired of seeing me draped sleepily across the couch with my mouth hanging open, as I'm sure it has been. The thought of doing this five more times doesn't excite me, but I know I have to push through.

September 18, 2014

Day 7

Two steps forward, one step back. I felt so good yesterday, that I tricked myself into thinking I was over the hump. Today, nausea has crept back just a bit. I was warned that it could come out of nowhere at any time. Also, after viciously fending off constipation, my colon has gone fiercely in the opposite direction, and I can't stray far from the bathroom. Still feeling pretty good, but I'm back to slow and steady. Marking the days off as if from a prison calendar. Just keep looking to the finish line. I have never wanted to rush to Christmas quite like I do this year. Final chemo just after. I will celebrate New Year's by being done with this part of the battle.

September 19, 2014 (10:18am)

Day 8

Pump it up, pump, pump it up! That part of a song came to mind this morning while I was waiting in the doctor's office. Began my day with Dr. B. getting a saline fill. Working toward my new "girls". I will say this again and again because it bears repeating, I am more than grateful for the awesome doctors on Team Woods. I'm just one patient of many to them, but every visit I'm made to feel like I'm the most important. I've never felt like a number; no one ever should. If you don't get that kind of treatment from your doctor, get a new one. You need to have total faith in them. I do! I'm putting my faith in them to save my life and make my body whole again. Plastic surgery appointment over, now headed to oncology.

(12:11 pm)

Appointment number one today was a snap, number two, not so much. My port did not want to cooperate. Last week, I had to lay down to facilitate drawing blood from it. The tech remembered that and so I started today lying down. That didn't work. She had me turn my head to the right. No. Lift my left arm over my head. No. Sit up. No. I felt like I should get up and do the Hokey Pokey. She had to inject me with something to dissolve whatever was blocking it, wait 20 minutes, and try again. That did it! Yay! Blood was drawn and I was hooked up. Infusion of Herceptin only today. I get that with chemo, but doc wanted a couple of extra doses in the beginning. I'll do this next week, too. Another step toward the finish line.

(12:52 pm)

Sitting here in the infusion room and someone across the way just completed her treatments. She got to ring the bell and then the nurses gathered around clapping and singing, "Hit the Road Jack". How cool! I'm teary just sitting here watching it.

September 20, 2014

Day 9

I am finding it helpful to look at breast cancer message boards to get direct info from those who have been through it. It's one thing for a doctor or nurse to tell you what should or might happen and the best way to take care of it and another to hear what actually happens and what helps from someone who's been there, done that, and lived to wear the t-shirt.

Thursday night I started having some pain in my lower back. I knew it was the result of the Neulasta shot that I got on Monday. That is the shot that stimulates the bone marrow to ramp up white blood cell production. The most common side effect is bone pain and body aches, which pretty much signify that it's working. Friday, my back was starting to hurt more and by evening, my legs and hips were killing me. I was moving around like someone twice my age. The nurse had told me to take Ibuprofen for the pain, that didn't touch it. This morning I woke up with my whole body screaming from a deep ache in every bone. I had read several conversations of survivors talking about Neulasta pain. It was mentioned several times that, for some reason, Claritin seems to help. I took one this morning and within half an hour, I felt like a new person. Another odd, inexpensive, helpful hint. I bought the generic store brand and it worked just as well. It is wearing off now and my legs are both throbbing once more, but I'll try it again tomorrow and hope it works the same way. It was truly like night and day. I have learned some quite helpful things from message boards, blogs, and being in touch with survivors themselves. If I didn't have that help from the Claritin, there's no way I could have gone out with my son tonight to take Homecoming pictures.

Neulasta is used to increase the formation of white blood cells, which help to fight infection. Some types of chemo can deplete your white blood count and decrease the body's immunity. Infection is a definite enemy at this time and needs to be avoided at all costs. The pain that may result from Neulasta can feel crippling. I was thankful to find a useful tip within the survivor community to lessen the misery and make it tolerable.

For future treatments, I would start taking the Claritin the day of the shot and continue for the next week or as long as needed. At the time, no one could define why it worked, but further reading explained that Neulasta may also cause the release of histamines that are linked to bone marrow swelling and pain, so it makes sense that an antihistamine would be an aid. It might not be a good idea for everyone, but it worked well for me.

I do feel that the Neulasta was a great addition to my treatment plan and worked as it was meant to. I was not sick with any colds, flu, or infections during my treatment period. Once I had finished chemo and was no longer on the Neulasta, I ended up with a terrible cold that took forever to kick. It's easier to get the shot now that they can send you home with an attachment that injects you without having to make a trip back to the doctor. That sure would have been helpful. My chemo treatments were on Friday, so I would go back in for the shot on Monday. By that time, I was so sick I would be practically crawling into the cancer center. Treatments are improving and evolving all the time.

The other thing of note in this post is about getting out to take Homecoming photos with my youngest son. I was feeling a bit weak and mildly achy, but I put on my big girl panties, and I was there. It was his freshman year of high school and it already seemed like I was missing things. Over the next months, I would come to feel like an inadequate mom, and it weighed heavily on me.

I was fortunate to have been a stay-at-home mom to my boys. The stay-at-home description is a bit of a contradiction, but that's another discussion altogether. From the beginning, I was there with them for everything, be it home activities, playgroups, or playdates. When they got to school, I was the mom who volunteered for it all. I was at every party, decorated bulletin boards in the hall, helped grade papers, assisted in organizing fundraisers, went to the PTA meetings, and drove for every field trip, even when my son asked me not to drive because he wanted to ride with someone else. Eventually, I even ended up going to work part-time at their school. With few exceptions, I was there.

Admittedly, some of that was for me. I wanted to experience and hold on to every piece of their childhood knowing that it wouldn't last forever, but I also wanted them to know that I was there and always would be. My involvement had started to slow in junior high when I went back to work full-time, but I was still present as much as possible.

When Sam got to high school, we were entering the last leg and I wished to remain involved. I knew it was all coming to a close and wanted to hang on till the end. He was also at my alma mater, and I thought it would be fun to be there on the other side. As it turned out, it didn't go quite that way. For most of his first year, all I could do was catch up with him from my spot on the couch. I returned mostly to myself before his freshman year wrapped up, but I had missed so much and wasn't connected to anything. It wasn't what I had hoped for and is one of the things that I regret the most about the timing of the whole cancer inconvenience. I hope that he knows I was there as much as I could be. As it turned out, he was the one who ended up being there for me. When the tide turned, both of my boys stepped up.

ON POINT

September 25, 2014

I got back to work this week. Feels good. I was met with many hugs and have been told multiple times that people are happy to see me and have me back and that I was missed. Very genuine and heartfelt sentiments. Made me feel good!

The office didn't collapse while I was gone and they can clearly survive without me, but it was nice to be welcomed back with such enthusiasm. I am fortunate to work with a wonderful group of people who I feel are my extended family. I'm also extremely fortunate to work for a company that is caring toward their employees and with management that has been amazing through this. I know that not all employers are as gracious. I'm just glad that I remembered how to do my job. It was like riding a bike but without the uncomfortable seat and bumps in the road.

I'm merely doing half days currently and that's all I can handle, by 11:00 am I'm wearing down. I'm feeling good right now, but still, tire quickly and my body gets achy. I need to make the most out of this week before my next treatment. I know what to expect now and how to deal with the ups and downs after, so maybe things can be a little smoother the second go-round.

September 26, 2014

Let's talk about nipples. Ha-ha! Now I have your attention. If you're not a teenage boy, this is a subject that you don't likely think about or talk about often. If you're a breast cancer patient doing reconstruction, it's something that requires careful consideration.

The first decision you get to make is whether to keep your own. They can perform a "nipple-sparing" mastectomy that does just what it says or a total mastectomy that takes everything including the nipple. Choosing to keep your nipples may sound like the thing to do, but there are a couple of things to greatly consider. Retaining yours means leaving some amount of breast tissue, even though minute, it's a risk. The other issue is that they must be reattached to the blood supply and that may not be successful. If it doesn't work, the tissue can die, and they would be lost anyway. If the tissue dies, it may turn black, and the nipple can even fall off. The risk of returning cancer or dead nipples falling off my body didn't sound appealing, so I chose not to go that route. Whether you keep your own or have new ones created, as mentioned before, they won't have any sensation. That part of the dance is over. No more feeling in the breast area. At this point, what's the next step? There are basically two choices; have them included as part of the reconstruction or don't and go on without them. I had assumed that I would have them included in reconstruction, but I feel like I have more to think about. It seems there are a few different ways the reconstruction can be done. It can be created from the new breast if there is enough skin or donor skin is taken from somewhere else on the body, which means another surgery and recovery. If they are added this way, later, tattooing is done to provide the color for the nipple and areola. It's more procedures and more time healing.

Another option is not to rebuild them but to have 3-D nipple tattoos done instead. That would provide the appearance but eliminate more procedures. An advantage to bypassing reconstruction is that I could go braless on nearly any occasion. There would never be an intrusive nipple protrusion under a tee shirt or anything else. I hate bras! That has long been an item to be shed nearly the moment I walk through our door. I'm a master at unhooking and pulling it through one armhole and out the other. My boys have gotten so used to this trick that they don't even blink at it anymore. Since I usually enter through the kitchen door, it would not be uncommon to find my bra draped over a dining chair. If anyone stopped by unexpectedly, I would have to make a quick visual sweep to be sure there wasn't a boob harness anywhere in sight.

The thought of not having to wear a bra is enough to carefully consider doing tattoos instead of the reconstruction. Maybe I'll be more creative than just tattoos of nipples. I could get a couple of daisies or smiley faces. It's an odd subject, to be sure, but one that requires me to make a big decision.

HAIR TODAY, GONE TOMORROW

September 30, 2014

And so, it begins...my hair is coming out in volume. I'm preparing myself to rock a bald head. It makes me feel sick to simply run my fingers through my hair and come away with a collection of dark, errant strands. When I wash my mane in the shower, I end up with a wad of hair that could be mistaken for a small rodent. Not sure why, but I'm still using conditioner in my washing routine.

My hair is everywhere! Yesterday I gave Sam clean gym clothes for school. He told me that when he went to get dressed, he pulled at least five black hairs off his white shirt. All I did was carry the clean, folded shirt to his room and that much transferred. Eric then added that he found one of my hairs draped over his finger when he was beginning to put his contacts in yesterday morning. It's time for the mess to go. I need to rid myself of it before our drains are clogged or I end up with random bald spots and look like a dolly who has been abused and had her hair pulled out. It will be a relief to be rid of the constant fallout. I think my scalp will feel better, too. It has been sore and a little itchy.

I'm okay with the thought of my new hairstyle or non-hairstyle. It will be an opportunity to play around and have fun with different looks. I stopped after work and picked up a couple more hats to add to a pink one that I already have. I also have a wig, a couple of scarves, and several beanies that were lovingly knitted for me. I have lots of options. I may even decide to embrace my baldness on occasion. I was thinking that I could use markers to write and draw on my head. I might put inspirational messages or jokes, cartoons, or flowers, or draw in hair. I even thought I could rent it out for advertising and make a little money off it. "Your logo here," for a price. Just a thought. Time to go; got an appointment with some shears. Update to come.

Here's the story on the wig. I started looking at wigs thinking it was what I needed to do. I thought maybe I would find one that looked like me and I could pull it off like I had hair. I wasn't sure if I would wear it, so I didn't want to make a big investment.

The American Cancer Society has a program that provides free wigs to cancer patients. Our local cancer institute houses this program and has a room full of wigs to choose from. I went in, tried on several, and found one that I liked and thought looked good on me. Funny thing was, it looked like a "Rachel" cut from the TV series, *Friends*. That was funny because Jennifer Aniston, who played Rachel, is Eric's celebrity crush. I was okay with that. She's a mature woman (translation: my age) who seems down to earth. Besides, it's not like he was going to run into her somewhere and have the opportunity to take off and be her "boy toy" in Hollywood. To be fair, I have my own celebrity crush in Hugh Jackman. I have made it known to my family that if he ever shows up at our door, I'm out! No worries, that would never happen. But, hey, Hugh, if you're reading this, "What's up?" (Wink, wink!)

Anyway, his love of Jennifer Aniston may have played a little into me trying that one on, but it did look cute. It was sandy blonde, but I was wanting to stay with my more natural dark color. Not even sure what I was thinking there. If ever there was a time to try something different, that was it. They didn't have it in my color, so it was ordered for me. How cool is that?! Not only do they give you a wig for free, but if they don't have the size or color that you are looking for, they will order it for you. It is a wonderful thing that these programs exist to assist cancer patients with finding pieces of their normalcy. I didn't end up using the wig much. I became comfortable in the scarves and head wraps.

October 1, 2014

It was a family affair last night when I went in to shave my head, Eric and Sam joined me. We went to my mom's hairstylist who I've known since I was a kid, and she knew my mom through both of her bouts of breast cancer. Eric shaved his head with me. Sam didn't wish to shave his all the way and I would never want him to, he has beautiful hair. He wanted to do something, though, so he shaved the sides down. I let them go first.

It was a trip to see all of my hair go away, but it's a relief. Now I don't have to watch it fall out. It was on my terms. I look a little like Sinead O'Conner right now, for those who remember her. Anxious to see what my cue ball head looks like when the remaining stubble falls out. I'm glad to see that it isn't too misshapen. I do have a dent on the top of my head near the back and a scar from a junior high mishap with some monkey bars and a metal slide. Cracked it wide open! Anyway, it's not bad. I will embrace it for the next several months. Accessories will become my friend for sure! Many people told me at work today that I can pull it off and should just rock my bald head. I may sometimes, we'll see.

It was emotional watching the clippers gobble up my hair. Not in a million years had I dreamt that I would be taking on a shaved head. Never was there a "Britney Spears moment" when I thought bald would be the way to go.

GIRLS JUST WANNA HAVE FUN AND CHEMO

October 3, 2014

Chemo #2

Second chemo today and I'm riding it out with my head exposed. When today is complete, I will be one-third of the way done. I'm embracing my "GI Jane" look to go with my warrior spirit.

An excerpt from the life of a breast cancer patient:
During chemo today, I was invited and encouraged to feel up a stranger and I did.

Toward the end of my treatment, a woman, her daughter, and her husband came and sat in the pod area next to us. At one point, I passed them on my way to the bathroom and the lady, who was hooked up to her own magic liquid, stopped me and asked where I got my shirt. I was happy to share where I purchased my fuchsia, Under Armour, Pink Warrior shirt, since I work there. We chatted for a moment, and I went on to take care of business. Later, I noticed that she was covered under a blanket with pink ribbons printed on it. I commented that I guessed we were there for the same reason and that sparked another conversation.

She had completed chemo after having a bilateral mastectomy. She was there for Herceptin treatment like I will do after my chemo, to complete a year. She mentioned that she will have her reconstruction surgery on Monday. My reaction was to blurt out how lucky she was to be getting rid of the dreaded expanders. That led to talk about the expansion process and how they feel. Her adult daughter was saying how her mother's boobs are very hard since they are fully expanded. I didn't realize they would be that way. At that point, the woman told me that I could feel them. I said, no, that was okay, but she insisted. Okay, so I felt the side, quickly. What do you know, it was pretty darn hard! Now I have a special connection to this warrior sister who had been a stranger just an hour earlier. I never know what my days will bring in this strange reality.

I would like to tell you that was the only time that I felt up another survivor, but that would leave out my inspecting a friend's expanders. When you become a member of this pink sisterhood, things like that can be commonplace. You think nothing of talking about boobs, looking at them, even touching them, or showing yours to someone else.

Along those same lines, there was the time that a close friend and fellow survivor and I were sitting outside of the Olive Garden. This is the same friend that I mention feeling up in the paragraph above. With the restaurant ready to close around us as we continued talking after dinner, we decided to move our conversation to the bench outside. We had been talking about reconstruction and options; I was past mine while hers was still to come. I thought nothing of showing her pictures of the nipple tattoos on my reconstructed breasts. I'm quite proud of them, as they are truly impressive. I have pictures on my phone and have shown them before, but usually just close-ups of the tattoos. With her preparing for reconstruction, I showed pictures of the whole shebang. (Details on the tattooing are in an upcoming chapter.)

As we sat there on the bench with our backs to the parking lot looking at pictures of boobs on my phone, a male employee suddenly walked around from behind us and into the building. We cracked up at what he must have thought of the two middle-aged women sitting outside on the bench looking at boobs. Good grief, what did he think? We both found it a perfectly natural action until the stranger walked up. That was a moment that definitely required context. He will never truly know what was happening outside his workplace that night, but I'm sure his imagination created its own ideas. I hope that he laughs to himself if that picture ever surfaces in his mind like I do when I think about it.

On another note, at my second chemo appointment, I brought along a prayer shawl that a dear friend had made for me. I stayed comfortably enveloped in it for the duration. This is not only special because my friend thought enough of me to gift it, but also because the lady who made it said prayers specifically for me while she was creating it. It is literally infused with prayers, good thoughts, and best wishes for my health and recovery. To this day when I wrap up in it, as I do on occasion, it feels like being cloaked in love.

October 12, 2014

So, I started out thinking that the side effects from this second round of chemo weren't as bad as the first, I was wrong. They are lasting longer this time and I'm getting frustrated. In the beginning, things went smoother. Nausea and fatigue didn't hit until later Saturday and weren't as intense. That lasted through Tuesday, then, just like before, I felt really good on Wednesday. I went back to work and thought I was in the clear. Wishful thinking. Thursday, I felt awful again. Back to nauseous, very weak, and feeling the effects of loose and frequent stools that had started on Wednesday.

Turns out, this time, the loose stools are the worst of it. I will call it that rather than the "d" word, which just seems a bit more off-color, but you know what I'm referring to. It's not a pleasant subject, or usually one for public talk, but in the interest of putting it all out here, that's what's been happening for four days now. What goes hand in hand with the loose stool problem is irritation of my hemorrhoid friends below. If you are familiar, then you know the pain. Of all the changes that childbirth brings, this is one of the worst. At 8:00 am yesterday, I was already using the sitz bath. If you don't know what that is, you're lucky; if you do, I'm very sorry. Let's just say that I never thought that I'd have to sit my butt in a bowl of hot water to try and find relief.

Weakness and body aches are coupling with that issue to tick me off. I don't want to just lay around, but that's about all I can do right now. I'm missing out on fall, my favorite time of the year, and it doesn't seem like it's going to stick around too long. For me, the loss of complete independence is one of the worst parts of this whole thing; not being able to do what I want to do because my body won't let me. I guess I'm a little bit of a control freak and I'm not in control right now. It's not just affecting me; it affects my family and what I can do for and with them.

We had to cancel a planned date night last evening and that's not fair. I need to be able to do more with my husband than lay next to him and whine about how crappy I feel. He just kisses my forehead, rubs my back, and tells me it's okay then asks what I need. I am so very lucky to have this man in my life. Timing is everything. It wasn't the best for him, but I was blessed with the support that I needed just at the time I needed it. We will celebrate our first wedding anniversary two weeks from today. This year has brought big challenges, but it has shown me the worth and strength of my partner.

I was using Zofran and Compazine for the nausea, but the combo didn't completely take it away. I was cautious of using them too long because one caused constipation and the other diarrhea. Nice, right?! With bowel issues being one of the biggest problems at that time, I didn't want to push it. I threw some Imodium into the mix and that helped to keep things running smoothly, so to speak. I knew there was the possibility that side effects would get worse as I went along but was determined to use what I learned each time to lessen them the next. It helped to remind myself that there were only four treatments to go.

October 24, 2014

Chemo #3

I'll be at the halfway point after this one. Woohoo! I can see the light at the end of the tunnel, and it is looking beautiful. I was given a new hat at chemo today. Now I can be a spiky blonde when I need a change. It's fun and it's nice and warm. Jake thinks it makes me look like Guy Fieri from the Food Network.

Some lovely soul made a bunch of hats in different colors and brought them to the infusion unit to be handed out. They were crocheted with additional yarn that stood up on the crown to create a bit of a spikey hairdo. I chose pink with blonde spikes. You never knew when you might come in to find a treat that had been dropped off to be shared with the chemo patients. It could be cookies or hats or possibly something else. I wouldn't have thought of it before I became a recurring customer of the liquid buffet, but it's worth mentioning.

If you are looking for a group to spread joy to via your baking, knitting, crocheting skills, or otherwise, your local cancer treatment center is a good place to share the love. Anything for a patient that can make the hours they spend being infused more comfortable will be appreciated, especially during the holidays. Think hats, scarves, lap quilts, blankets, or light treats. A small pillow that could be slipped under the back of the neck, held against the chest, or lightly snuggled, can be a soft comfort. The nurses in the unit can also use a little extra sunshine for days that, I imagine, can be extremely challenging. During such a trying season of life, small gestures hold big meaning. All during my time as a cancer patient, during treatment and recoveries, I was blessed by people who went out of their way to make my hardship easier. That human connection is a soul-changing gift.

WHEN THE CHEMO GETS TOUGH, THE TOUGH KEEP INFUSING

November 14, 2014

Chemo #4

I'm two-thirds of the way done. It's nice to be looking at only two more. I will be happy when I can get my body and life back. The only thing that makes this easier is the flood of love and support all around me. I am so very thankful for my family, friends, and coworkers who care for me, comfort me, check on me, call, text, and send cards. My youngest son also shows support by regularly wearing pink. He wore pink every Friday in October and every time that I've had chemo. There was one October Friday that he didn't have school, but still wore his, "I wear pink for my mom" shirt to the football game that night. Today he was sporting pink socks and that same shirt. He went to a party tonight in both. Representing for his momma! The visual support is a nice comfort.

October had an extra special feel this year. I have always acknowledged and supported Breast Cancer Awareness Month and already owned many items adorned with pink ribbons, but the whole meaning was different looking at it from the other side. Every time I saw someone wearing pink or something tagged with a pink ribbon, I felt support from strangers and the community at large. One Friday, I was heading to the clinic for my treatment and drove past the construction area at the hospital. Crossing the street just in front of me was a big, burly, bearded construction worker wearing overalls and a bright pink shirt. That brought an instant smile to my face. The lamp posts around the clinic buildings during the month also sported large, metal, pink ribbons. Lovely, glaring, public signs of support.

I have always loved pink, though. When I was younger, I had a pink bedroom the color of Pepto Bismol. When I moved into my current home, the master bedroom was a shade of pink, too. My husband knows that I enjoy getting random flowers and all the better if they're pink. On my desk at work, you will find pink push pins, pink post-its, pink pens, a pink note holder and pen cup, and my favorite, a pink high heel tape dispenser. My cubicle is also still decorated with the pink signs of encouraging words that the girls put up for me before I left for surgery.

A newly diagnosed breast cancer patient said she was told, "I hope you like pink because from now on you will be surrounded by it." I do and I don't mind being surrounded by it. I wear pink ribbon-adorned items whenever I can or a cute pink rhinestone ribbon pin. I have done this for many years in support of my mom and other family members, but now I feel like it clues onlookers into why I'm wearing a scarf or hat indoors and why there's no hair peeking out from underneath. I have had people who notice the ribbon and whatever is covering the sparse, black sprouts on my otherwise balding head ask me about my situation then they tell me their own story or about a relative who has gone through something similar. The conversation usually ends with them saying they will pray for me or encouraging me to hang in there. It's nice. There is, without doubt, some true evil walking around our planet, but I think that most people, at the core, are good and feel for others, even those they don't know. I have seen that quite a bit along this journey. We are all connected through our collective experiences.

A cashier at Schnucks brought me to tears a few weeks ago. It was a pink October Friday, and I ran down to the store to pick up toilet paper and a couple of food items, some of the few things tasting okay at that time. I was wearing a shirt with a pink ribbon on it, a jacket with a pink ribbon, and a scarf on my head covered in little pink ribbons. It was getting late, and the checkouts were empty. I got in line, set down my purchases, and was greeted with a smile and questions of how I was doing, and if I found everything alright. It was a night that I wasn't feeling well and I'm sure it showed. The cashier asked if I was a survivor and I told him that I was in the middle of it and going through chemo. He said that he felt for me and knew what I was going through then proceeded to tell me his story.

In 2005, he was diagnosed with Non-Hodgkin's Lymphoma. He underwent twenty chemo and radiation treatments that put it into remission. A couple of years later it came back, and he went through a stem cell transplant. It was hard and he said he questioned why him, but he made it through and is in good health now. He told me to keep going and I would get through it. He said he would pray for me, and I believe that he probably did that night. That encounter put things into perspective for me. When I get down and frustrated with feeling bad and want to quit, I think of that cashier at the grocery store. If he could persevere through all of that, I can certainly make it through the rest of my chemo. I also think of all the words of encouragement and love that come my way daily. I look at the cute cards that I am still getting, and I get strength again. Two more to go. Almost there!!

I believe I will always remember that grocery cashier. I was directed to his line that night because I needed that interaction, a little shot of perspective. He didn't have to talk to me and tell me something so personal, but he could see that I needed it. I have tried to extend the same to others when I can tell that they need it. We are all human and being human is hard, some times are harder than others. In those extra tough times, a few kind, unifying words, and some encouragement can make even that which is awful more tolerable.

I still see that cashier down at the store. He is always smiling and friendly. One visit last year, I mentioned to him about the conversation that we had that night. I inquired about his health, which is still going strong, and let him know that I was well, too. I thanked him for speaking up then and wished him well.

December 5, 2014

Chemo #5

Just one more after today! A great way to end the year.

December 8, 2014

I know I only have one treatment left, but right now it feels like it's forever away. I can't wait to regain some

147

control over my body. It's frustrating to get completely worn out doing the simplest things. I'm not sure I remember what normal even feels like.

December 9, 2014

I'm becoming increasingly concerned about possible long-term effects from chemo on what was an otherwise healthy body, to begin with. Side effects are increasing, and new ones are popping up. My fingers and toes are becoming more numb and they ache, my fingernails are starting to hurt and so are my teeth. I would love to hear from any of you who have been through this as to how things turned out. I'm trying to make a decision and some input from those who have been through this may help.

The decision I was trying to make was whether to go through with the final chemo treatment. I had come to a point where I didn't want to do another one, even the last one. A big issue with the three-week space between treatments is that you have the chance to start feeling better before it's time to go back. The process was that I went for chemo, started to feel bad within the first two days then felt awful for about five days, began to feel a little less awful, and swing back up to feeling acceptable that third week to the point that I walked into the infusion center with a smile on my face and feeling good. The problem here is that you go in on the upswing knowing that within a few days you're going to feel like hot trash again. I just didn't want to do it!

I was also beginning to worry more about the damage that I was doing to my body that may remain after it was all concluded. It took a few treatments for side effects to build and worsen and seem like they could cause irreversible damage. The body pain that I was starting to experience was also a worry. My joints ached. My appendages were starting to hurt, and my toenails were beginning to lift off my toes a bit. The fact that my teeth hurt was a real concern. I was afraid that they might fall out. I don't know if that happens and I doubt it would after just five treatments; even so, it worried me. I felt like maybe I should stop and take my chances. After all, I had gone through five treatments, that had to be worth something. How much difference could one more make? I know that is flawed logic, but that is where my head was. It's difficult when you are back to feeling good to willingly walk into a situation that you know is going to make you sick.

Thankfully, I had a friend who picked up on what I was contemplating and knew better. She enlisted the help of a longtime breast cancer survivor friend of her own to bring me back to my senses. I got a call out of the blue from Franci, an amazingly sweet human being. She talked me through it. She said she knew what I was going through and how I felt, but that I knew that I needed to finish it. I did know that. I'm not sure why I was trying to convince myself otherwise. As Franci said, if I didn't finish it and then had a recurrence, I would always blame myself and wonder if it could have been stopped by that final date with chemo. I needed to complete it and be done. Wrap it up in a bow and move on. That talk pushed me back on track and, once again, headed me in the right direction.

Strangers are just friends we haven't met yet. Many strangers made huge impacts on my life during my hardest journey. I am indebted to them all.

WE WISH YOU A MERRY CHRISTMAS AND A CHEMO FREE NEW YEAR

December 25, 2014 (12:18 am)

Finally laying down. So happy to be in my bed instead of at the ER where the doctor wanted me tonight. I noticed that my ankles were a little swollen Monday when I got home from work. Tuesday, they got worse. When I woke up this morning, my feet were swollen, too. By late morning, I had no visible ankles. The tops of my feet were so swollen that I could feel the fluid in them, and my calves were starting to join in. When I called the oncology office, they sent me to Prompt Care. We spent two hours of our Christmas Eve afternoon there.

It was noted there that I have gained nine pounds in the last week and a half. I have had a few Christmas goodies, but not nearly enough to explain that. I'm clearly retaining a lot of fluid. The first concern was possible heart failure. Blood work and a chest x-ray ruled that out, as well as kidney problems. The clinic doctor called the oncology office and the doctor on call wanted me in the ER for Doppler scans of both legs to check for blood clots. It would be very rare to have them in both legs at the same time, but he has seen it and didn't want to overlook anything. After celebrating Christmas with my mom, we prepared to spend the rest of our night at the hospital. I just didn't want to. I called the doctor, and he agreed to let me try Lasix for a couple of days to see if it would eliminate the fluid. I will go in on Friday for the Doppler scans. Every day is a new adventure. I never know what my body will do next. I feel like, "I got 99 problems...".

December 26, 2014

Doppler scan was normal, no sign of clots. Good news, but no explanation for swelling and no relief. Guess I'll chalk it up to poisoning my body and keep my feet up.

December 29, 2014

While I was Christmas shopping this year, I was given an unexpected gift by a stranger. A lovely woman was dropped into my life to give me just what I was needing. It wasn't a coincidence by any means, more divine intervention. That was one of many instances where someone was put into my life at the perfect time. Those happenings help to affirm my faith. I completely believe that God puts the people in our lives that we need at the times that we need them.

Six years ago, we agreed to become a host family for the local junior hockey team. It was something that my first husband felt we needed to do, but I was a bit apprehensive. I had two young, impressionable children at home and was unsure about bringing in a teenage stranger. I didn't know what kind of influence this kid would be on my boys. I changed my mind and wanted to back out but was told that we weren't going to break the commitment. I prepared for our new housemate but felt some anxiety. That anxiety went away the first night that our guest arrived.

The player that came to our house was polite and friendly and fit in the moment that he crossed the threshold of the front door. We could not have asked for a better influence for our boys and addition to our home. Brandon became an instant family member. Three weeks later, my husband of sixteen years walked out. He had been contemplating it for several months but waited until we had taken on this additional responsibility. I remember thinking about how I was not only left to singularly care for my two boys, but I also had someone else's son in my home to look after and care for. Thanks a lot!

That turned out to be a huge blessing. In the face of a horrible, earth-shattering situation, a teenage hockey player who had been a stranger three weeks earlier, became our saving grace. That nineteen-year-old kid helped to keep me and my family from completely falling apart. He took our minds off of things by getting us to play games or watch movies or get out of the house. He became a big brother to my boys and someone that they could talk to. He was also someone that I could talk to. He became my third son. His family would visit a weekend or two each month and stay with us and we became close to all of them. Collectively they helped me survive one of the worst situations I had faced.

A funny side note here is that a lot of people knew that I had separated, but few knew that we were housing a teenage hockey player. When I started showing up places with this unexplained, handsome, young man, I got more than a few sideways looks and some questions from those who were brave enough to ask. That doesn't have anything to do with my point, but it tickles me. We are still in touch with Brandon and his family, and I know that there will be a lifelong bond. He even shaved his head after I did in support of me. The kicker behind all of it is that he was not the player that we were set up to host. There was a situation and at the last moment, the very day he was to move in, they switched players on us. The player that we were set to host was just about the opposite of the one who moved in. I have no doubt it would have been a completely different experience with the other teammate. That was not happenstance.

Another person who came into my life at the proper time married me. We had no idea when we walked down the aisle of the huge challenge that we would face less than nine months later. Us ending up together was something that almost didn't happen. There was a point early on before we were officially dating that Eric nearly balked, but I'm persistent and wouldn't let him leave the game. Later, we hit a bump in the road and things temporarily went off course. Thankfully, we realized that we needed to travel together. There was a purpose to getting past those near misses.

I could not have made it through the past five months the way that I have without this man by my side. He has been my rock, my strength, my comfort, my main support, and my biggest cheerleader. He has kept me going and helped me know that it will be alright. He has seen me at my worst but still gives me his best. He kisses my bald head and embraces a body that has been a mess. He is the one that I needed to get over this gigantic mountain in the road. I can't begin to describe how thankful I am that he is with me. There is timing at play here; again, no coincidence.

The two biggest challenges of my life have been made easier by the right people appearing at the right time. Sometimes there are small examples of this, too, like the woman that I encountered shopping. I have been struggling with the side effects of my last few chemo treatments. That has made me doubt my decision to go through with the "preventative" chemo and is causing worry about the damage that it is doing to my body and what of that might be lasting. I have done a lot of reading on the computer of survivor stories and people talking about after chemo looking for examples of lasting effects on survivorship. Most of what I have found and even people who I've talked to are short-term or just a few years out from it all. That doesn't answer the long-term questions that I have.

I was shopping the week before Christmas and was wearing a hot pink cap. A woman was passing me and told me that she liked my hat. I smiled and thanked her and went on. A little later, we came side by side in an aisle and she stopped me and again told me how much she liked my hat. She said that I really looked good in it, and she wished that she looked good in hats but didn't feel like she did. While we were standing there talking, she must have noticed that there was a lack of hair sticking out from under my cap in any direction. She suddenly asked me if I needed to wear a hat. I told her that I was going through chemo. She then asked where I was in my treatment, and I told her that I had just one left. She said she knew what I was dealing with, that she had been through it.

Twenty-nine years ago, she had breast, uterine, and lung

cancer. She was an attractive woman who looked to be in her sixties and in good health. When she told me that, I teared up and said, "God bless you." What a huge thing to face. I asked her if everything that she lost during chemo came back for her. She said that everything came back except for her eyebrows. She didn't have numbness and her taste was fine. There was one thing that she was still unable to eat, but otherwise, no problem. I asked if everything was good with her, and she said that it was. She was a sweet lady; her name was Ruth. Ruth asked my name and said that she would pray for me. I walked away with the relief that I needed. I had just talked to a near thirty-year survivor of a much more difficult cancer than mine who had come through it all and had no lasting problematic effects from chemo.

I was only in that store because I was wasting time after dropping the boys off to Christmas shop for me and it was the closest place to be outside of the mall where they were; turned out it was just where I needed to be. You never know when a blessing in human form is going to drop into your life. Sometimes they are meant to be there for a moment or just a short while, others are meant to stay by your side. Be grateful for them all.

December 30, 2014 (9:53 am)

Chemo #6

For three and a half months I've been waiting for this day, my final chemo. Hallelujah!!

There is still more to my treatment, but this nastiness is ending. I'm expecting about two weeks or so of feeling not so great and then let the healing begin. I've finished the first leg of the race; thank you all for coming along with me!

(4:42 pm)

This is a milestone day for me, and I wanted it to special. Started my last chemo with my hubby by my side, then my Aunt George came to finish it with me. It was so nice spending time with her and I'm happy she could be a part of this. Additionally, I planned to go out with my boys and honey for dinner tonight and to a movie that I've been wanting to see. Trying to get a couple of things in while I still feel good. A nice day, for sure, but in between, there was another little surprise.

After treatment was over, my aunt and I went to Baker's Square for a celebratory piece of pie, because what better way to kiss nastiness goodbye than with a piece of Lemon Supreme Pie. A woman from a nearby table came over to us as she was leaving and put a card down for $5 off and asked if we could use it. It was expiring tomorrow. That was a very sweet thing to do. She was having lunch with her daughter and I'm sure they could have used it on their meal. I'm guessing that she noticed my pink ribbon scarf, earrings, and "pink warrior" shirt and wanted to pay it forward to someone going through a tough time.

When our server came back to bring the check, we inquired if we could use the card. She asked when it expired, and we said the next day. Our server looked at us and inquired if we could come back then because today was on her. She laid down our "check". It wasn't a bill, instead, she had written on it, "It's on me girls! Have a great day! Fight like a girl!", with a heart and her name, Shelby. Instant tears. George looked at me and told me to tell her my thing. I said that I just finished my last chemo treatment, which made it even better. What an awesome thing to do. A blessing from a young waitress. Before we left, we thanked her again and she came over to hug me. There is still good in people; we need to focus on seeing that instead of the bad and being the light out there for others. Today, Shelby was another little angel in the form of a stranger along my journey.

TEN THINGS I HATE ABOUT BREAST CANCER AND EIGHT TO BE THANKFUL FOR

December 31, 2014 (11:17 pm)

I am reflecting on this past year as it ends. I can honestly say that there has only been one other year that I was as happy to see end as 2014. That year was 2009, and I ended it at midnight by hurling a small gold band as far as I could from a friend's balcony into the snowy expanse of the backyard. It was very therapeutic. I will say goodbye to this year in a much quieter way, by sharing a kiss with my husband of fourteen months who has ridden the ups and downs with me.

The year started normally but took an ugly, unexpected detour in July. The months that followed have taught me much, both positive and negative. I have learned that cancer is a vile disease. Not that I didn't already know that or that other diseases aren't equally as horrible, I've just learned about this one firsthand. Cancer sucks! It is a thief that comes out of nowhere and robs you again and again.

In the case of breast cancer, it begins when you get the phone call that your mammogram shows something new that needs to be checked out. That is when it **starts stealing your time and sense of security**. Time is taken with worry and then with the various doctor appointments. Once the diagnosis is confirmed, it starts robbing you of your sense of security and brings a question of uncertainty to the future. It makes you face your mortality and worry about what will happen to your children.

Then comes surgery and that unceremoniously **takes your boobs**. These can be replaced, of course, but the reconstruction process can be drawn out, painful, and is uncomfortable all along the way. I will be as happy to say goodbye to the expanders in my chest as I am to this whole year. My chest has been expanded to the point that I have what resemble small breasts, but they are so hard that the resemblance is strictly visual. The likeness is there when clothed, not so much when nude due to the three-inch scars across each side and lack of nipples. I'm confident that I could knock someone out with these babies if I was to hit them in the head at the right angle. Currently, they are more safety devices than female enhancements.

If you have the pleasure of going through chemotherapy, the theft continues. It took your boobs, so next, it **takes your hair**. There's nothing quite as attractive as a boobless, hairless woman. I was fortunate enough to find a man who seems to be able to deal with it. It wasn't in our marriage vows, so I might assume some kind of fetish I wasn't aware of. I didn't go completely bald, though, some random hair remains and has continued to grow during my good weeks. The result is sort of a cross between a deranged person and a baby orangutan. Baby orangutans are adorable, though, so I don't mind the comparison.

Next, it throws you into **temporary menopause,** steals your libido, and complicates bedroom activities. Just perfect for a newlywed couple. This might be the point where you find out what your husband is truly made of. Mine is made of awesomeness!

While this cancer thief is picking your pockets, it **takes your strength**, but generously leaves behind **nausea, neuropathy** in your hands and feet, **excessively watery, twitching eyes,** and **fluid retention**. One of the worst things it takes is your **sense of taste**. Most foods don't taste as they should, and some are just inedible. But never fear, it leaves behind its own version of a horrible metal taste in your mouth that is there constantly.

These are most of the things that this process has gotten from me. Others have different experiences, and some are much worse.

The Bible tells me to give thanks in all circumstances and so I shall.

I am thankful first and foremost for a faith that has given me comfort and helped to carry me through this.

I am thankful that my cancer was caught early and successfully removed by the hands of one of the best surgeons in the field.

I am thankful that I am working with a top-notch plastic surgeon who will restore my chest.

I am thankful that chemotherapy exists to wipe out possible remaining cancer cells and hopefully inhibit any future growth of this cancer in other areas.

I am extremely thankful for our healthcare system and the wonderful people and facilities that I have been privileged to during all steps of my treatment.

I am looking forward to, when my hair returns, trying new hairstyles that I would never have had the courage to cut my long hair short enough to try.

I am thankful that the expectation is that the side effects should all wear off and my body should return to what I knew as normal.

I am also unendingly thankful for the love and support that I have been surrounded by from the start.

Now, bend over 2014, so I can give you a giant kiss goodbye. I head into 2015 on the upside of treatment ready for healing and rebuilding. Happy New Year!

AN EXPANDING RESISTANCE AND THE LASH REVOLT

February 3, 2015

Well, I owe you all a post and I'm sorry that I'm about a month late. I need to give a bit of an update. I have had a lot of people asking how I am, and I want you to know that I'm doing well. It's been a month since I completed chemotherapy. Things are starting to come back. I have a bit of neuropathy remaining in my fingers and toes, but I'm hopeful that will go away, and I will regain full feeling. My eyes have finally stopped watering excessively and they're not twitching as much now. I'm thankful for that. People thought I was crying all the time. I was saying something to my fourteen-year-old one day about being frustrated with all the watering. He said that he had wondered about that and thought that maybe I had just become overly emotional. I have tiny hairs sprouting in the bald patches on my head and, unfortunately, on my legs and under my arms, too. That's kind of a downer. I have enjoyed not shaving these past several months.

The worst side effect remaining is the pain and weakness in my legs. The muscles in my thighs ache and burn all the time. Walking upstairs or long distances is tough. I did a little research on this and found out that one of the chemo drugs that I had, Taxotere, is very hard on your muscles. I got a real taste of that recently at my cousin's wedding. I wanted to dance but could barely make it through "The Cupid Shuffle" and "Shout" was challenging me. Throwing my hands up, kicking my heels up, and getting low during "a little bit softer now", was proving very difficult. My body isn't all the way back yet, but I'm generally feeling fairly good. I appreciate so many people asking. The reconstruction part is not progressing as well as hoped, though.

My chest muscle is too tight and not stretching as it should. The expanders are rock hard, which can present an interesting situation. I got a lot of hugs at the aforementioned wedding and some of them were pretty tight. I detected a hint of confusion in a few of the huggers when my chest assaulted theirs. Typically, when you hug a woman, you don't expect to feel two cement mounds pressing back against you. The lack of stretching of the muscle and skin puts limits on what can be done in the size area. There go my hopes for getting that second job at Hooters. My doc and I have decided to halt the injections since they're not doing anything but causing more discomfort.

Surgery is scheduled for May. To get a better result in reconstruction, I will need a bit different operation than originally planned. Instead of a simple exchange of the expanders for implants, I will have latissimus dorsi flap reconstruction. That involves having areas cut out of each side of my back that will take skin, tissue (aka back fat), and muscle and move it to the front. That move will take place by tunneling beneath the skin under my armpits to sort of slide the cut-out flaps around through the inside. That allows them to remain connected to their original blood supply. The back flaps will be used to add tissue to the breasts and build them up more. I'm assuming the muscle that is used will provide form and support. Putting tissue over the chest muscle will also make the new breasts softer. Implants will be inserted, as well. This will require four areas of incision, four drains, and a longer recovery. It's also going to add more scarring than I was planning for, but guys dig scars. No, wait, chicks dig scars; not valid. Oh well, every scar tells part of your story.

My story has sure changed in the past six months, my husband's has, too. Little did he know that he was signing up for a Frankenstein monster project where parts would be taken from here and there and pieced together to rebuild his wife. Saying that just brought three things to my mind, the movies *Young Frankenstein* and *Weird Science* and the T.V. show *The Six Million*

Dollar Man. From *Young Frankenstein,* I'm thinking that I'm glad the parts will be my own and not come from Abby Normal. I think I only thought of *Weird Science* because they built their ideal girl and named her Lisa. I'm not ideal, but I am a girl named Lisa. From *The Six Million Dollar Man,* I'm hearing, "We can rebuild her." Just call me the two hundred-thousand-dollar woman, so far anyway. In short, I'm feeling good and thankful for all who have been asking and all out there who have been so caring along the way.

When I went to the plastic surgeon for my expander fill in November, I overdid it a bit and soon lived to regret it. I popped in there feeling good about how well things were going and ready to pump it up, even more, to reach my goal faster. I told the doc that I wanted to put extra in, and we went for it. The remorse was quick. Fills usually included some discomfort, but this came on fast and didn't go away. I don't remember if it was the same day or the next, but I was rapidly in so much pain that it brought me to tears. It was just before Thanksgiving, but I was less than thankful about the repercussions of my choice. I quickly decided to stop fills for a couple of months. I decided I was fine with the size they were at and whatever bra cup I could get out of it at that point would suffice. It wasn't worth the pain to keep going. When I visited the doctor and she confirmed that the pain was from the failure of the muscle to stretch, my surgery type changed. I was happy to be done with the fills and excited to get to the surgery and beyond.

March 1, 2015

The cancer trip includes, at no extra charge, a continual emotional roller coaster ride. The real fun is that you never know when the coaster is going to turn or take a sudden drop and there is no hint as to when it will stop so that you can get off. You may think your ride is coming to an end, but then it gets going again. This ride will also cause occasional trips to the pity potty, where you typically sit alone, not to be confused with a pity party. I like that term. It's one that I found used on a cancer message board. Those message boards have been very helpful. Reading that other people have the same experiences and feel the same way brings comfort. A survivor made the statement that it's okay to take a turn on the pity potty, but don't overdo your stay. You know, if you sit there too long, you start to go numb. I have tried not to visit the pity potty very often, but I've been there a few times. I thought I would share my most recent visit.

I never actually went through the whole "why me?" thing. I didn't look at it that way because I had expected it. In my family, breast cancer seems to be part of the legacy. Anyway, I accepted that it was my turn to deal with this disease and went about the business of taking care of it. Big things like "why me?" haven't sent me over the edge, it's been much smaller stuff. One night, after my surgery, I lost it because the cat wouldn't leave me alone and I couldn't move to get away from her. The cat who was by my side comforting me the whole time, who I love like crazy. I know it's just accumulations of feelings. I have tried to be positive most of the time, but now and then I slip backward. My most recent slip was around two weeks ago and only my husband got to enjoy it. Lucky him, he gets all the fun. What sent me hurtling over the edge? Eyelashes! That's right, eyelashes, or more accurately, the lack of.

When I settled into the decision to go ahead with

chemo, I resigned myself to losing my hair. My oncologist told me that was guaranteed. I didn't want to lose my hair, but it was going to happen, and I would find ways to deal with it. I have gotten a bit tired of finding ways to cover my head, though, and am looking forward to styling some hair again. Occasionally I forget that my head is not completely presentable. Last week, I started to leave for work and realized when I stepped into the garage that my head was bare. It was below freezing that day, so the cold aid tipped me off. I wonder what I would have done if I had gotten all the way to work with a bare head. That experience is probably why I had a dream recently that I was at work with my head bared and trying to play it off. It was like the dreams I have previously had about showing up at work or being on the way to church wearing a skirt and realizing that my legs weren't shaved. As a pale skin person with dark hair, those were more horrifying.

I sometimes find myself getting interested in a new hairstyling method that I see in a magazine or a new product and then I remember that it will be a while before I can do any follicular styling. It's getting close, though. Maybe a few more weeks and I'll be ready to face the world with a close-cropped hairstyle. It seems to be filling in fast. In a couple of weeks, my white scalp with random hairs dotting it has become considerably darker as new hair is sprouting and filling in among the scraggly longer hairs that shoot straight up. I still have that baby orangutan kind of look if I don't push the long hairs down, but it's coming along. I've gotten a little off track, back to the missing eyelashes.

At the beginning of this journey, I said that I would be okay losing my hair if I got to keep my eyelashes and eyebrows. I feel that my eyes have always been my best feature. I was blessed with long black eyelashes and great full brows. Thick, full, Brooke Shields kind of brows with a nice, natural shape. In high school, I had a male friend who called me Betty Boop because of my long, dark eyelashes. I never left home without mascara on to make them even longer and darker. I always felt ready to face the world as long as I was wearing mascara and a little lip cover; my two essentials. Like American Express, I never left home without them. My mom is going to see this and not be happy with me, but I couldn't even begin to count the number of times that I have applied mascara while driving. I know, that's not a good thing to do, but I'm quite a pro at it. Since I'm coming clean, I'll also admit to having batted those dark eyelashes at a few members of the male species along the way. It may have helped to further my cause a time or two. I'm sure my husband can attest to that. I've batted in his direction more than a few times.

As I've gotten older, I've noticed that my lashes were a little less than they used to be, but they were still great. Now they are all but gone. I don't understand how I managed to keep them all through chemo, but now that I'm finished with that and my hair has started growing back, my eyelashes have deserted me. They had thinned, but there remained plenty just a few weeks ago. My eyebrows had thinned, also, then began getting bald spots. I had to start filling them in with eye pencil at the beginning of February. I can see, though, that they are beginning to grow back. I'm already back to tweezing random hairs to keep them under control. I didn't miss tweezing at all. Even though I had managed to keep my lashes and brows for most of the time, there was no other hair on my face. Yesterday, for the first time in months, I had to take care of things on my upper lip and a few randoms on my chin and neck. You ladies know what I'm talking about. If you men don't, then your woman is successful at keeping it from you. For those ladies, sorry, your secret is out. I need to have a pact with one of my close friends that if I'm ever incapacitated, she promises to tweeze where needed so that I don't end up with a mustache and goatee. Any volunteers? That is what my son would call oversharing. Sidetracked again!

A couple of weeks ago, I visited the eye doctor about this thing that I had in the bottom of my eyelid that was causing redness, swelling, and pain. The kind of thing that when you go to work, co-workers look at you and ask, in horror, what is going on with your eye. That's what happened and what sent me to the eye doctor that day. Before I knew it, he had some sort of torture device prying my eye open and was cutting on the lower lid, inside and out. I could hear the snipping. I'm so glad I couldn't see any of it and mostly couldn't feel it. I have blepharitis and he removed a chalazion. The oil glands on that side have backed up and are causing swelling, inflammation, and pain. The result of that little office surgery was a black eye that started before I even left the building.

As I stood in the mirror that night checking out my first ever black eye, I noticed that all the lashes from my lower lid on that side were gone. Sorry, no, there is one left. Uno, single, lonely, one! I had still had lashes on that lower side. I didn't have many on the other side, so I stopped using mascara on the bottom lashes earlier, but I still knew they were there and that gave me comfort. Now, they were gone. Somehow, during the eye torture fest, they were removed or just ran away in fear. That really torqued me off! Then, I looked at my other eye and realized that a whole gang of lashes from the middle of my upper lid on that side were gone. Where did they go? They were there that morning. Now, nothing.

I stood there looking at myself and saw that I could nearly count the lashes that I had left. About ten in the corner on one side and maybe fifteen scattered on the other. In lash amounts, that might as well be zero; they were all but gone. I peered in the mirror at my black eye with a cut under it, two bare eyes with no lashes and a sparsely covered, baldish head, and it was too much. The chemo is over, I'm supposed to be coming back. I got in bed and lost it. I complained to my husband about how unattractive I had been feeling, and now, I had lost my eyelashes, the one thing that I had fully hoped to hang on to. As my sweet husband laid there trying to say things to make me feel better, I cried. A lot! He finally gave up and just held me. I know it must be difficult to be the man dealing with the crazy woman. Here is a quote that my husband has borrowed and directed at me, "Always love a woman for her personality. They have like 10, so you can choose." He's right, I don't deny it. When you come to terms with that, you, your spouse, and all your personalities can live happily together. Anyway, he went to sleep, and I cried. Do you know the worst part of that? Crying makes your eyes swell. Do you know how hard it is to try and hide swollen eyes without eyelashes or hair to camouflage or distract from them? I do.

In the grand scheme of things, I know that losing one's eyelashes isn't the end of the world. There are so many more important things to be concerned about and focused on. I also know that it wasn't only about eyelashes. It was a buildup of things and that was just the eyelash that broke the camel's back. It was more about wanting this all to be done so that I can move on. It was about tiring of all the doctor visits and being poked and prodded and having my eye cut on. It was about trying to hold on to an appearance that used to be more youthful than my actual age and that I feel this experience is stripping away. It was about not wanting to appear older than my younger husband. Calm down, there are only six years between us, so I'm not officially a cougar. It was about the loss of control that comes with the cancer fight. It was silly, really. There is so much worse in this battle, and I don't wish to demean any element of it for those in it. For me, right now, the hardest piece is over, and this is where I am, crying over eyelashes. It's part of the crazy ride.

Since then, I have realized that maybe it's good to be stripped of your ego at times; it reveals the raw person inside. I have no eyelashes to hide behind or bat to get my way. It's just the bare me. The thing about that is, if I don't get a glimpse of myself in the mirror, I forget. I still feel like me. People still interact with me the same way. They still smile at me at the grocery store and strangers talk to me when I sit next to them. My smile is the same, my demeanor is the same, the people who love me are the same. It's all good! I still make up my eyes and, some days, even put mascara on the few little hairs sticking out the corners of each lid. I'm making what I can of it. Not gonna lie, though, I can't wait to have my lashes back! Crazy as it is, right now, I miss them more than my boobs. How weird is that?! I have never claimed to be fully normal.

GONE TODAY, HAIR TOMORROW

March 12, 2015

Big step tonight, went out in public without my head shrouded. Dinner out, even. Very liberating! It feels good not to have my head smothered with a covering. No one looked at me sideways and my husband wasn't embarrassed to be with me, so I'm about ready to set my head free on a daily basis. I think I'll wait until next week for the big reveal. It needs to be trimmed up in a couple of places. Funny thought, I know, but there are some longer hairs here and there that need to be trimmed. The hair is filling in well and seems like it's growing more every day. Exciting times!

March 15, 2015

Okay, today's the day, let's talk about hair. Hair is and, long has been, a big part of our lives. Consider stories and legends about hair, like Rapunzel and Lady Godiva. There is even a Broadway musical simply named *Hair*. The title song talks of wanting a head of beautiful hair. Ultimately, the musical isn't about hair, it's about the sixties, but that was a time in history that separated people by both their political views and by how they wore their hair. Hairstyles punctuate certain periods in time. Finger waves denote the 30s, pin-up rolls evoke memories of the 40s, the 50s brought us ducktails, long-haired hippies and beehives scream 60s, while Farrah Fawcett feathers bring to mind the 70s, and big, permed, back-combed, over-sprayed hair, helps you remember the 80s. Then there's the mullet, which maybe shouldn't exist at all. People use hair to express themselves in all sorts of ways.

If you want to show rebellion, you can shave just one side or sport a pointy mohawk. Dye your hair an unexpected color to show your adventurous or uninhibited side. Some people hide behind their hair. You can put it up to be serious or formal, or let it down to be sexy. Cut it short to be sassy or grow it as long as it will go. You can curl it, twirl it, braid it, weave it, wave it, shave it, put it in a bun, fashion it into a pigtail, a ponytail, or a fishtail or just let it be. My point is that hair plays a huge role in how we present ourselves and how we are perceived. To that end, losing your hair alters that and vastly limits your options. You can say, "It's only hair", and yes, that's true, but it is a large part of who we are. It takes serious adjustment to suddenly not have your locks. The only good thing about losing it to chemo is knowing that it is eventually going to come back.

It was very exciting when my hair started growing and filling in. It's nice to see less and less scalp as more area is covered. The regrowth process is kind of symbolic. It's brand new, baby hair, a fresh start; a new beginning after chemo, after cancer. It was about six weeks after the final chemo treatment that I noticed sprouts of hair in the bald areas. At two months past, it was noticeably filling in. At this point, I have enough hair to feel comfortable baring my head to more than just my immediate family. My husband and sons have been privy to my head in all stages of balding glory and have remained mostly sweet about it. I can't say that the boys haven't teased me a little, but they are teenagers, and I wouldn't expect anything less. I have laughed along with them, especially during the crazy mental patient stage of random growth. They have petted my head and told me that I can pull off the bald look. My wonderful husband has rubbed and kissed my head on a nightly basis and excitedly tells me how much my hair is growing. He has cheered me along in all areas and done everything he can to encourage and lift me up. The way that he has embraced my new hair has given me the boost to expose my head at this point. It's a great relief to go without a smothering cover. I feel free!

I got a little haircut today. The men in my house teased

me about it, but it did make a difference in how it lays down. The wild ones needed to be tamed. It's been five and a half months since my head was shaved and I sat in the rotating seat at the beauty salon. I have enjoyed saving money by not buying hair products and preserving countless hours that would have been spent fixing my hair, but I'm anxious to give that up. It will still be some time before I need to use more than a drop of shampoo or put in more than a couple of minutes to style my hair, but that time is on the horizon, and it feels good. I'm excited to experience different hairstyles that I would have never had the courage to go for on my own. The beauty of starting from scratch is that I have an ever-evolving canvas to work with. Before, I wouldn't have had the nerve to try a pixie cut, but you better believe I will have one when my hair fills in a tad more. I may even try a shag, and, at some point, there will be another bob. For now, I will rock my baby hair. Let the fun begin!

NEWLYWED GAME - CANCER VERSION

I didn't talk about this in the blog but felt it was worth including in the book. Chronologically, this is where it belongs.

Eric and I married in October of 2013. By that time in the year, neither of us had much work vacation time left and so decided to hold off on our honeymoon until October of the next year. The plan was for a cruise around our first anniversary. The advent of chemo put that on hold. The doctor would not sign off on allowing me onto a boat full of people carrying who knows what kind of germs that could wreak havoc on an immune system that would be diminished by that time. Additionally, it was likely that I wasn't going to be feeling too well, so we canceled the fall cruise and found one very similar in April of 2015. Chemo would end the prior December and we were banking on me being well enough to travel by then.

Things went as planned and, by April, I was ready, willing, and able to embark on a cruise up the western coastline. It was a great trip, and we had a phenomenal time, but that isn't why I'm telling you about this; I wanted to share a funny story that had a lasting, positive result.

Activities were taking place all around the ship each evening. One night we decided to check a few out. We joined our in-laws, who were also on the cruise, in an area that was hosting multiple games. One competition was a version of The Newlywed Game. We were chosen to participate as one of three couples. We were the most newly married couple at about a year and a half. I don't remember the timeline of the other couples, but one had been married for several years and the other, an older couple, had been married for quite a long time. The outcome of this participation is both comical and produced an interaction whose result remains today.

I remember only three questions, one of which wasn't any big deal, and two that resulted in both comedy and mild embarrassment. It worked just like the old game show; first, the men went on stage to be asked questions about their wives or married lives and give their answers to the audience then the wives came out to answer the same questions to see if the responses matched. After completion of that series, the men left the stage, and the wives had their turn.

Here are the two questions whose responses were mildly unexpected, to say the least. I'm not sure whose question this was, "What color underwear is your wife wearing?", but we both got the answer correct; I wasn't wearing any. That calls back to an encounter with my doctor that I told you about previously. The audience wasn't quite ready for that one and, remember, my in-laws were there, as well. The other notable question was a bit more confusing for the host and included an uneasy truth.

Eric's question was, "What is your wife's bra size?" I think the focus was on the cup size. It seems like a simple question, but really, how many husbands are sure of their wife's bra size? Do they even know how they are sized? I feel like it's something that they don't worry much about or have an interest in knowing. My husband has never bought me a bra and doesn't do my laundry, so I'm not sure how he would know. Perhaps he might have noticed the tag on one of them hanging in the bathroom or slung over a chair like I mentioned earlier. I suppose if you are quite busty, wearing an E, F, G, or above, your man might know this so that he can brag to his buddies about it. I don't know, seems like something men might do. No shade, just my feeling. Do all women even know how bra sizing works in that the number is the size of the band and the letter the cup? Anyway, I'm certain that my husband had no idea what my bra cup size would normally be, but these were not normal times. I don't recall how he answered, but it was my answer that caused confusion.

When asked my bra size, I sat there for a minute trying to figure out what to say. The host was looking at me like I was nuts when I told him that I wasn't sure how to answer the question. He quizzically asked how I wouldn't know my bra size. I answered that I was a breast cancer survivor who was in between surgeries and didn't currently have an actual bra size. That stunned him momentarily. It was the same deer-in-the-headlights reaction that I had seen before on people who were hit with me casually blurting out my cancer status and catching them off guard. When he snapped out of it, he congratulated me and uncomfortably continued to Eric's answer, which, of course, didn't match mine.

We ended up having the most matching answers to win the game and were gifted a bottle of champagne. As we left the stage, a lovely woman with an English accent approached and stopped me. She said that she was also a breast cancer survivor of some time and I think she appreciated me speaking up. We talked briefly, she was sweet, I thanked her, and we all left, as game time had ended. The next day, we boarded a bus for an excursion to end up sitting in front of the same charming woman and her husband. We had a conversation acknowledging having met the night before. I think I asked if they were following us or said we were following them. Not sure, but there was some stalking comically inferred. There were other interactions during the outing, and we traded names to connect on Facebook, which we did. To this day, Pamela and I are Facebook friends and still in casual contact. You never know which situations will bring about lasting human connections. Don't be afraid to put your struggles out there; there may be someone right in front of you who can relate.

WE CAN REBUILD HER

May 14, 2015

The time has finally come for my reconstructive surgery, in the morning just a few hours from now. When this all began, I expected to be doing reconstruction by November. That was six months ago. The best-laid plans, right. Chemo derailed the process and prolonged the wait. I have had these awful expanders for nine months now and I will be more than happy to have them exit my body. Since my chest didn't expand as expected, they are extremely hard, and my skin is stretched very tautly over them. The skin is so tight that it's shiny. On Mother's Day, we were out to dinner with my mom and discussing the upcoming surgery. There were comments about how hard my chest currently is and how odd it feels to be hugged by me. There was also talk about the surgical procedure and implants and size, etc. My son commented on how strange it must sound to someone listening in who didn't know what we were talking about. Well, that's what they get for eavesdropping. It's so natural for me to talk openly about it that I don't even think sometimes about how other people may perceive it. This is my life now and I've become comfortable with sharing it. I am not ashamed to say that I am anxious about this surgery, though.

I wasn't nervous going into my mastectomy, but this has me a little on edge. I think the first time I was just so ready to get the cancer out that I was excited to do it. I had never had surgery before and didn't know what to expect. Now, I know what some of the recovery is going to be like and I'm not looking forward to it. I'm also nervous about the part that I don't know, the healing of my back muscles after being cut. If you have been following along with me for most of this, I have discussed details of the surgery before. It's not simply replacing the expanders with implants, it's a much larger endeavor. When I was at the pre-op visit last week, my doctor was asking how big I'm wanting them. At this point, I don't care; just give me something that resembles boobs again.

Once I am fully healed, I can add nipples to complete my new girls. I have previously discussed some of the odd decisions that breast cancer patients have to make, including those about nips; to keep your own or reconstruct or leave them off or just tattoo them on. I have decided to go with 3D tattoos. They will look like they're there, but they won't give away when I'm cold and I won't have to wear a bra to hide them. With a new chest that is pert and perky and nipples that are tattooed on, I won't need to be enslaved by a bra. The tattooing will have to wait until everything is well healed and things have settled. It would be a mistake to do it too soon and end up with them in the wrong place. It wouldn't be good to have one up near my chin and the other pointing toward my belly button. That's not the next step, though, time now to concentrate on the task at hand. I will be home by tomorrow evening with a newly built chest. One step closer to putting this all behind me. Like the shirt that I wore today says, time to "Keep calm and fight on".

May 15, 2015

Surgery went well. We got home about 5:30 last night. My time in the recovery room was longer than expected. I had difficulty waking up from the anesthesia. It wasn't a medical problem; I was just extremely groggy and out of it. I was like that all night and still a little bit this morning. I know that I was asking weird questions and couldn't keep my thoughts straight. We may have missed that great YouTube opportunity that Eric has been waiting for. I'm in my spot and thankful, once again, for my reclining couch. It's perfect since I need to stay propped up. Having some pain this morning, but not terrible. My pain meds are set up on a regular schedule. My honey even set an alarm so he could make sure that I took some before bed. I have the best nurse!

May 16, 2015

Post-op Day 2

Keeping pain in check with medicine every 4 hours. It hurts the most when I try to get up because it pulls on my chest and that's when I especially feel it. I'm the sorest under my arms today. That is from the tissue being tunneled through the armpits to get it to the front. Overall, the pain is not terrible as long as I stay seated. I have no pain in my back incisions but am laying against two extra-large cold packs at all times.

The whole drain thing is interesting. It takes longer to deal with four of them and I've had some leakage around where the tubes enter my body. One of the drains has a large, weird clot in it that is like a Jell-O Jiggler. If you've ever seen or made the egg jigglers at Easter, that's about what it looks like. If you aren't familiar with those, just trust me, it's kind of gross. It's also too big to squeeze out the little hole, so we have to work around it. The doctor says it's nothing to worry about.

Found it difficult to sleep all night sitting up, but I'm not supposed to lay down. I'm itching all over from the pain meds; Benadryl is helping some. While we were on vacation, I found a telescopic back scratcher that looks like a little rake attached to a pointer, it is becoming my best friend, and it is, of course, pink. The plastic one with a hand on it that I used the first time had broken. I'm feeling pretty good but am anxious to see what is under the big bandage compressing my chest. It feels great to have the expanders out, but I want to see what has replaced them. I know there were limitations since my muscles didn't stretch as they should have.

May 17, 2015

Post-op Day 3

Nothing new today, pretty much a replay of yesterday, but I'm more coherent. Some mild pain when I move, otherwise, just discomfort from the drains and swelling. With the four, plastic, bulb drains pinned to my chest and the tubes going from them into my skin, I look a bit like a science experiment when my top is exposed.

When it is all covered up, because the drains stick out and hang down, I look like I've got some stretched-out girls that I could tuck into my waistband. My underarms are still sore, and my range of motion is limited.

When I get sat down, I'm fairly committed to my placement, because rearranging is difficult. We've got a good method figured out for getting me up, which I do every few hours to use the bathroom, take a walk, and maybe eat something. My helper places both hands behind me and pulls me forward until I get where I can stand; similar to the method used during my initial surgery. All three of my guys have had the pleasure of doing this. We change the ice packs each time I get up, too. This requires someone to get them into just the right place behind my back as I sit down because once I'm down, I'm not moving. In order to get all the way to the back of the couch, I bend one leg, sit down on it, and lean back. Then my leg is stuck under me, and I need help pulling it out. What fun!

The hardest time is in the middle of the night when I need to use the bathroom, and everyone is asleep. Getting myself up at that point is both painful and comical, much like after my mastectomy. I slide toward the edge of the couch and push myself up, then, while I'm mumbling because it hurts, I'm having to fend off the cat who keeps trying to get back onto my lap to lay down.

I am relying on my guys most of the time and they are taking good care of me. I was concerned about this recovery, but I think it's not going to be terrible as long as I stay down and rest as much as possible. Because of my vicious independence, it's hard for me not to want to do everything for myself. At this point, there are things that I can't do, and I have to ask for help. I'm trying not to be demanding, but they seem to be okay with it. All of them have helped get me up, get me food, and cover me up. I'm generally feeling good, a little sleepy from the meds, but that's okay because I know that I need to rest. Having some very strange and vivid dreams when I do nap. Things keep showing up in multiples of four. Wonder where that is coming from in my subconscious and what it means.

I'm still very anxious to see what is hiding behind my bandage. There are a couple of sores on my stomach that are unexplained, so I need to find out what those are about. Looks like maybe something was taped there, and skin was pulled off when removed. Strange to not know what happened. That's the weird stuff that you don't want to think about. When I went into the surgery room, they told me to go ahead and lay down on my back and they would flip me over when I was knocked out. I don't want to think about how that went down. I have watched plastic surgery shows on TV, where, when working with the chest, they prop the patient up to take a look at how everything will hang and make sure they're even. So, there's that, too. I know the doctors and nurses are all professional and focused on the work, but it is still odd to think about being moved around into different positions while asleep and exposed. There was a good vibe going into the surgery room, though. *Lucky Star*, a Madonna song from the 80s was playing. That one brings up good feelings from my high school days. I took that as a sign that it was going to go well. It's all uphill from here.

May 18, 2015

Post-op Day 4

Had been feeling good today until about an hour ago. I have been able to get up by myself and don't have much pain. The drainage has slowed, and the swelling isn't bad. Four days of constipation were finally, thankfully, relieved. I realize that those four days were a blessing, since, until today, I wasn't able to reach where I needed to take care of that situation. That is not something that I wanted to ask for help with. I was horrified enough this morning when I noticed that my husband could see me plucking the hair from my upper lip, no way was I going to ask him to wipe my butt.

I have rested well all day. When I got up this last time, I

started feeling light-headed and nauseous. I haven't eaten much today and that's probably why. With all the meds that I'm taking, I'm sure I should pay more attention to when I'm eating. Settled back down with fresh ice packs and going to rest again. That's the continuing theme here. Starting to tire of it, but that is my job right now. Aside from the recent wave of feeling a bit sick, I think that I'm doing well. My reach is getting better, and my strength is good. Traveling down the recovery road.

May 19, 2015

Post-op Day 5

More than ready for this to be over. Nausea stayed with me through last night but subsided by morning. It came back for a couple of hours this afternoon then dissipated. Aside from that, I physically feel fairly good. I don't have pain, things are just a tad uncomfortable when I move or get up, which is very rarely.

When I called the nurse this morning with drainage

totals, she suggested that I must be doing more than I should because one of the drain totals had gone up. I was told to move my arms as little as possible. That would be so much easier if it actually hurt, or I wasn't able to move them much. It is difficult not to do something that you want to when you have the ability to do it. My son offered to help me out by duct taping my arms to my sides; I passed. The desire to get these drains out by Friday is enough to force me to comply and only move my arms when I absolutely need to, this includes eating, taking a drink, or using the bathroom. Petting the cat and typing on my phone with one finger, are actions that don't require much movement, so I consider those freebies that I can do as much as I wish.

So, here I sit trying not to move. Five days in this same spot are starting to get to me. Hopefully, there will only be two more to deal with. I'm not tired enough to sleep my time away. Starting to get weepy, fighting it as much as I can. Just another twist on this crazy roller coaster.

May 22, 2015 (12:29 pm)

Getting ready to go to the doctor for the big reveal. After a week of no idea what is going on under the bandages, I'm anxious to see how my body has been modified.

(3:58 pm)

Back from the doctor. The drains are out, surgical bandages off, big compression bandage off and it feels wonderful! I am happy to say that I have a new chest that looks good even just a week after surgery. Dr. B. explained that it is a process to get them healed and formed and will be a couple of months before we see the complete result. For the next few weeks, I am to stay squished down as much as possible in compression bras and or wraps. This will keep the swelling down. After that, an underwire bra will help to give them form. Bonus, my back is tightened up where the tissue was removed, so that should eliminate that area of back fat at the bra line.

I still need to keep my back on ice packs and stay on the

good meds for the next week; I'll be home longer than expected. Better to do this right and heal properly. I won't be restricted to simply sitting and not moving quite as much, so I don't feel bad about taking it slow.

HIPAA, HIPAA, HOORAY!

May 26, 2015

I may have addressed this before, if so, I'm going to mention it again. I find such a laughable inconsistency with the issue of privacy we've created in the medical world. We have all these HIPAA (Health Insurance Portability and Accountability Act) laws to protect our medical records, and everything is held in such secrecy that it can be difficult and time-consuming to get needed information to your insurance company to process a claim. When the insurance company and doctor can deal with each other, it's fine, but when you become the middleman, it can get frustrating.

I watched a friend deal with this recently when she

required a form from her doctor that was needed to send to the insurance company. She asked the doctor's office to fax it to her, then she would fax it to the insurance company. The doctor wouldn't fax it because she didn't have the fax machine right at her desk. She explained that it was very close to her, and she would go and wait for the form and would be the one to receive it. Because other people had access to that machine and someone else might be able to see it, they wouldn't send to that fax. By asking them to send it to that machine, she was giving her consent, so I don't understand what the problem was. Instead, she had to take lunchtime and go to the doctor's office and pick up the paperwork; an inconvenience that shouldn't exist in our technological world when information can transfer from place to place in moments. They say it's a matter of privacy. I'm all for the option of privacy, but I think that a person should be able to open that up if they so choose.

Obviously, I can be very open about personal matters

since I've shared so much with all of you. I realize that others want much more privacy and don't wish to share personal things with those close to them, let alone strangers. That should be everyone's right. There are personal things that I don't want to be shared either but, if I request that a doctor send information to me on a public fax and I understand that someone else might see it, I don't understand why that can't be done. If I ask for my info that way and I know I'm opening up my privacy, it should be my choice.

I am currently dealing with this very same situation. Because my time off of work has been extended, I need to get information to the short-term disability insurance company. I contacted them and expressed that I was going to be off longer and was given instructions on how to extend my time. I was told that they would need the office visit notes from my recent trip to the doctor showing that she was extending my time off and why. When I questioned what was needed, they said to tell the doctor what they had told me, and the doctor would know what it was and send it. The insurance company said to have the doctor's office fax that to them.

I called my doctor's office and told them what I needed. They responded that they cannot send office visit notes out unless the insurance company requests them in writing, then I have to give permission to release them, then it has to go somewhere else. It's a much bigger process than just faxing over what I asked. Without all of that, the office can only send a very plain, standard form that says that I can't work until whatever date. It's the form they give you for school or work when you need to show that you've been to the doctor which has next to nothing on it. That's all due to HIPAA in the name of our privacy. I don't think that the insurance company is going to accept just this, but I said to go ahead and send it to maybe get things going.

Okay, no problem, except that the doctor's office can't fax that to the insurance company. Even though the form will have no information on it other than my name and the date that I can return to work, it can't be faxed from the doctor to the insurance company that requested it even with permission given from the patient. HIPAA, again. It will have to be picked up and then I can fax it to them. No problem, oh wait, I'm on medical leave and can't drive and I don't own a fax machine. My husband will have to take time to go pick it up and then find a public fax machine to send it from. I'm hoping that the form will be enough, but I'm suspecting that it won't be. The last time I dealt with this and needed to extend it, the person handling my case extended it on my word with no problem; this time, they're telling me they need office notes. Fingers crossed!

I said that, to get to the real issue where I feel the privacy inconsistency exists. I laugh to myself every time I go to a doctor and stand at the desk going through the very public interrogation. I give my name and they ask why I'm there. That is answered for all to hear, then I'm asked if I still live at the address that they blurt out.

Next, they ask if my phone number is still the number that they clearly state for everyone within earshot, both home, and cell, and do I still have so and so for insurance and am I still employed by such and such and my husband's name is this and my emergency contact is that and their phone number is what it is, and my primary doctor is who he is. Of course, they also ask my birthdate. That's my favorite because I love to announce how old I am to a room full of random people. Let's just complete this thing and bring the scale out to the front desk so we can get the weight out there, too. The only thing they don't ask is your mother's maiden name and what color underwear you're wearing. My point is, that a lot of personal information is freely shared during the doctor check-in process.

By the time I'm checked in, everyone in the room may know where I live and work and my phone number, if I'm married, how old I am, what other doctor I go to, and why I'm there that day, but don't worry, they have no idea what my blood pressure was at my last appointment or when I'm expected to return to work because HIPAA is protecting that. It's a stalker's dream.

I get that it's necessary to check these things to both verify that I am who I say I am and to keep information current and updated, but could they do it another way? Granted they don't always ask all of those questions, but in the interest of privacy, you would think they could maybe just hand you a printout of your information and have you look at it to verify its accuracy. Yes, that would waste paper, but after every appointment I have, I'm given a three-page synopsis showing why I came in, my weight and blood pressure, upcoming appointments, and current medications. The info could all fit on one page, but there are a lot of unnecessary lines and empty space. It's not anything that I need anyway. If I'm not given this at that time, then it's mailed to me. The medical profession does not seem to be worried about wasting paper.

All of my doctor appointments are through the same

clinic system. I see the same receptionists time and time again. They know who I am. At one point, I was in a clinic office regularly at least two or three times per week. Chances were pretty good that I hadn't moved and changed all of my information within the two days between visits. I would try to head things off by saying that nothing had changed, but they would still have to ask me questions. When I mentioned to the nurse today the irony in the fact that they couldn't fax what I requested, but they will freely spew out all of my info at every appointment, she said that if a patient has a problem with it, they can be taken aside, and it can be done in private. I don't have that much of a problem with it, and I'll answer these questions in public again and again, but I still find it a little perplexing. My medical information is protected like Fort Knox, but my personal information is laid out for public consumption like a smorgasbord.

To wrap this up, here's the punch line: My husband went to the doctor and picked up the paper that I needed.

Before he faxed it, he noticed something and texted me a picture of it. He was questioning if the form should be signed. The form only has three things on it; today's date, my name, and the date I can return to work. That's it. The doctor's name isn't even on the form, let alone her signature. Since the info on it is simply typed in, this could be a form completed by anyone. With them having asked for the doctor's notes from the office visit stating why I'm off of work longer, I'm fairly certain that this nearly blank form without a doctor's signature isn't going to cut it. I'll take the form when I go back to the doctor to get it signed and fax it to the insurance company. We'll see if they take it. Let the dance begin.

I know you're on the edge of your seat; surprisingly, the form was accepted. Literally nothing personal on it. I have also started answering my interrogation questions in French. Well, I would if I knew French, because wouldn't that be fun!

HAVE BOOBS, WILL TRAVEL

June 7, 2015

Here is a very small update that includes a funny encounter with a stranger. I felt it was worth sharing.

I'm doing well! Yesterday, I felt good enough to get out in the beautiful day and work in the yard. Wanted flowers, needed color, so I did a little flower shopping. Upon returning to my car, I noticed the car parked next to me was the same make, model, and color as mine. By the time I returned my cart and headed back, the owner of the other one was there unlocking it. I said to him, "Hey, I like your car." He smiled, then realized why I had said that. Because my car is the sport model, I have options that he doesn't. He started pointing out things on my car that he would like to add to his, like the spoiler and the V6 engine. Then he noticed the sticker in my window and said, "And yours has boobs." It is just the word, not a picture, but that is the word that stands out the most. So, I read the sticker to him, "Check your boobs, mine tried to kill me", and told him it was because I had had breast cancer. Pay attention to this next part carefully ... He said, "I'm sorry, did you survive?" Mull that over just a little.

I know that he, most likely, meant to ask if I was going to be okay. I have had that question posed before. I threw him off a little by just blurting out that I had cancer and he reacted quickly. It was funny. I answered yes and said that I had just had my reconstructive surgery. He said that it looked like they had done a good job. I got in my car and sat there for a minute replaying the conversation and laughing.

I answered, "Yes" to his question, which in itself is kind of funny. What if I had answered, "No", would he have even caught it? A friend suggested that I should have said that, yes, I survived, but my boobs didn't. I'm sure that he drove away scratching his head and wondering what just happened. I'm curious if he even realized what he said. I am not making fun of him; the situation was just funny and one that I'll remember.

I am the queen of saying things that don't come out correctly, especially in the era of, "That's what she said!" I live in a house with two teenage boys and a husband who sometimes thinks like one, so most of what I say doesn't come out right or just perfectly fits into that little mantra. I have been in this man's shoes and meant one thing but said another. This was the most perfect, "Here's your sign", moment that I've ever been part of. Hope that lends a little giggle to your day!

June 10, 2015

My husband and I haven't had many date nights lately because of surgery and recovery. I'm feeling good now and thought it was time to get out. We were kind of joking the other night when this came up, but then we both decided it had to be done. It only seemed right to go out and celebrate my new bra fillers by having dinner at Hooters. It goes with my theme of finding the humor in all of this.

I have never before set foot in one of their restaurants on the basis that I didn't feel the need to eat where there were a bunch of pretty girls running around in tight, skimpy uniforms. Maybe I thought I would feel inferior or maybe it was because of the notion that businesses like this objectify women. The reality is that the girls who work there are there of their own free will. They know the dress code when they apply. It's actually not that revealing. Everything is form-fitting, and the shorts are short, but they also wear tights beneath them. The shirts are low cut, but they are tucked in and fully cover everything except a bit of cleavage. I've seen more skin in other businesses when someone has bent over wearing low-rise pants and a too short, untucked shirt. That I find offensive. The girls were friendly and not at all inappropriate. I'm not trying to do a commercial for them, I'm just saying that it didn't make me feel bad about myself and wasn't the atmosphere I guess I thought it would be, it's a sports bar.

So, dinner at Hooters with, what else, boneless wings made with chunks of chicken breast. Appropriate food for the subjects being celebrated. I now know to be true what several males have told me before, they really do have good wings! I always thought they just said that for justification of going there. Nope! Who knew?! We had fried pickles and wings and I had iced tea because it is National Iced Tea Day in case you didn't know. When our server, Hannah, came to take the check, I told her that she had been part of our celebration of my new hooters. I was wearing a shirt that said "Support the Cure" with a big pink ribbon on it, so she understood what I was saying. She congratulated me a couple of times and then took our payment. When she came back, she had taken off the fried pickles as a gift of congratulations. Our new ticket had a note from her on it that said, "hugs and jugs".

She took that ticket with our payment, and I was disappointed when it didn't come back with the receipt. What she wrote was cute and I wanted to keep it with my collection of cards from the past year. As we were leaving, I asked her if I could get that ticket. It had already been shuffled off somewhere, so the manager was summoned to reprint it. While she was recreating her message on the new ticket, I was talking with the manager and telling him what we were in celebrating. He congratulated me and asked how things were going and if it was all good. He was also very nice, and his name was Eric, just like my hubby. I got my copy with notes, thanked them and we headed out. Just before we got to the door, the manager stopped us. He handed us a receipt showing that the credit card payment had been voided and said that dinner was on them. It was a very nice thing for him to do. We had a good meal in a fun way to commemorate a positive mile marker along this crazy journey and were shown kindness by two lovely people. It was a good night!

June 22, 2015

I am now about five and a half weeks post-reconstruction. I can't believe how quickly it has gone by. I am feeling great! Still a little tired, but I think that is mostly from a lack of exercise since surgery and I need to remedy that. I can at least drag myself onto the treadmill or get outside and walk if it ever stops raining. I had no real pain to speak of during recovery, only discomfort. I contribute my good experience to a fantastic doctor and surgical team, outstanding pain meds, great care at home from my three awesome men, the love and snuggles of my kitty, wonderful friends and family who checked on me and paying attention to doctor's orders while taking the time to heal and be a good patient.

I now have good range of motion with my arms and am close to full strength when pushing or pulling. I have a nice reach and force my stretch a little more each day.

I've gotten to where I can get to the middle of my back to scratch it but can't feel it if I do. The numbness is a very weird feeling. There is a bit more healing to be done, I think, where the muscles were cut in my back. The feeling of my latissimus muscle stretching from the back under my arms and around to my chest is still odd and will take more getting used to. It is tight, but I'm hoping that will change and it will become less noticeable. When I stretch my back, I feel it around my front. Certain areas in my mid-back are completely numb. My son finds it humorous to stand behind and poke me to see how long it takes me to notice. Teenage joy at my expense, one of the wonders of motherhood. I don't know how much of this numbness will be permanent. There is still a little swelling under my arms, as well, from tunneling the muscle through.

The back component of the procedure is most definitely the harder part to recover from, but it was needed and I'm glad that is the procedure that I had. With my chest muscle having been uncooperative, simply putting in an implant would probably not have given a natural-looking or feeling result. The tissue from my back has added both size and softness. I am so happy to have soft implants to replace the hard, uncomfortable temporary expanders that were there before.

Immediately after surgery, I felt relief from the removal of those expanders. They were something that I had an incredible love/hate relationship with. From what I have found in my reading and talking to other reconstruction recipients, this is pretty much the norm. The expanders are painful and hard and always uncomfortable, but they are necessary for this type of reconstruction. For that reason, I am thankful that they exist, but am also happy to bid them good riddance.

All four of my incision sites look good and are healing nicely. I did discover a stitch sticking out the other night from the corner of one of my front incisions, so I'm not sure what that means, but I see my surgeon next week. My chest is also healing well. I think I previously mentioned that I was told it will take about six months from the surgery for everything to be set in place and looking as it will. That would put it right around my birthday in August for final results; my present, I suppose.

Overall, I'm doing well. I have spent some time in front of the mirror, closely surveying my new landscape. I feel like things can't change that much in the next couple of months, so what I'm seeing is probably close to what it will be. Maybe I'm wrong and there will be some dramatic shift, but I can't envision it. What I'm sporting now looks great in a bra and kind of interesting out of one. If anyone other than my husband or doctor were to see me bare-chested at this point, they may be slightly confused at what they are looking at. The presence of the skin flaps and the absence of nipples paints a different picture than what most people are used to seeing.

I think my scars are going to be thin and blend well. I

welcome them because they are part of my journey and the road map of where I've been. They are mine and will be a reminder, when I notice them, that I have traveled around the roadblocks that were placed in front of me. I think that eventually, and probably rather soon, I won't notice the scars very much. It will be a matter of if I choose to see them or see past them. The scars on my back don't bother me; after all, I can't see my back and I don't expose it to anyone but Eric.

The one scar that is most prominent and visible to others, if the shirt I'm wearing is just a little bit low cut, is where my port is placed. I wear this scar proudly and feel joy when I see it. I don't look at it as something that has marred my body. It is a welcome part of this incarnation of me. It is a scar of major victory. It is my badge of courage and strength. It is the entry point of the chemotherapy that partnered with my surgery and other treatment that I'm trusting to have eliminated all of the cancer. The chemo was a battle of its own and I see my port scar as a hard-won medal.

The significant part of this is putting my body back together in order to feel whole again. Being able to see my nude body looking complete and normal, or my new normal will be an important part of healing. Every woman facing this has to determine what she needs to heal. It is a very personal choice and not to be made lightly. There are many options after breast cancer surgery and much to consider.

I have said before that I salute the women who can move forward without reconstruction, but I am not one of them. It doesn't make them any stronger or me any less, we just have different needs. It's like going through childbirth. Some women choose to do it all-natural, without any drugs, and even away from a hospital. That is their vision and how they want to take the journey. Me, however, I ordered my epidural as soon as I passed through the hospital door; I wanted as little pain as possible. I was still present and did the work, and it was no cakewalk. Going a different route didn't make me any less a tough momma and the end result was the same.

This is what I need to complete my healing. I didn't choose reconstruction so that I might forget or to act like it didn't happen, but to pick my life up where it veered off the natural course and continue moving forward. It's not like losing an arm or a leg, those appendages are vital and hard to live without, but there is a similar feeling of losing a part of your visible body. I am so very thankful that reconstruction is available and that now, rightfully, insurance covers it as part of breast cancer treatment.

For those who choose to replace their bosom, I'm happy to say that breast reconstruction is no longer considered merely cosmetic and now must lawfully be covered by insurance as part of treatment. Under the Women's Health and Cancer Rights Act of 1998 (WHCRA), if your insurance plan includes benefits for mastectomy surgery, it must also provide for reconstruction on the breast the mastectomy was performed on, as well as the other breast to bring symmetry. Insurance must also cover prostheses, should you need or choose to use them, and treatment for complications from mastectomy surgery. This act does not only apply to mastectomies due to cancer but includes those done for prevention or other medical necessities. Contrary to its name, this act extends to men, also. As of September 2020, this and additional information can be found on the websites for both the U.S. Department of Labor and Cancer.org.

I WILL SURVIVE...HEY, HEY!

July 3, 2015

It was one year ago today that my life veered off course and went down a new path. It would be six more days before I would get a confirmed diagnosis of breast cancer, but I knew when I saw the dark spot on the ultrasound screen, even before the radiologist asked me if I had a surgeon in mind. Much has transpired from that time.

Since this day last year, I have acquired four new doctors and have made at least 26 visits between them. I've had three surgeries; one to remove my boobs, one to place a port, and the last to put my boobs back. Those have resulted in seven surgical sites, the use of six grenade drains, and combined, have left nine scars. There will be one more surgery to remove the port in a few months. I have had three CT scans, three echocardiograms, and have had one nuclear-med injection. I completed six rounds of chemotherapy, received six Neulasta shots, and have endured eight additional Herceptin infusions with four or five remaining. I had two steroid injections into my eyelid and one procedure to cut a nodule out of it, which culminated in one black eye. I got a major haircut, shaved my head, lost the rest of my hair, started growing it back, and was thrown into early menopause. (Bonus – I haven't had a period in almost a year, downside – hot flashes and night sweats) I spent a total of nine weeks off of work, had about 25 meals delivered to my family, and was gifted three meals in restaurants; two by the staff and one from a friend who happened to be there dining at the same time. While all of that was going on, normal life around me continued, as well.

I celebrated my 45th birthday, my first wedding anniversary and we finally went on our honeymoon. My husband had a milestone birthday, completed a role in a local play and my oldest son turned nineteen. My youngest son started shaving, started high school, went to his first homecoming dance, had his first serious girlfriend, followed by his first serious heartbreak. He finished his freshman year, earned his driver's permit, and had his first performance in a local theater show. It was difficult to be sidelined during some of this activity, but I did my best to be as present as possible and enjoy all that I could.

It has been a busy year full of new experiences, not all of them good, but all are part of my growth. I have made many new friends and connections and have learned a lot about this medical journey and myself. I have new insights, a new outlook, and a drive to use what I've been through to benefit others. I am stronger, I am forever changed, I AM A SURVIVOR!

July 6, 2015

What an incredible day today has been! I was chosen as

one of three Super Survivors to be honored by our local hospital at their women's health fair in October. My friend/neighbor nominated me. Last week she was notified that I had been chosen and then secret plans were set in motion. With coordination from my husband, a group was pulled together that included friends, family, and a whole gang of coworkers who ambushed me at work, along with representatives from the hospital, Publisher's Clearing House style.

I was lured from my office under the pretense that someone was there asking to see me. That's not unusual, I have friends who come in the store and ask for me now and then. I had a passing thought that it was a little strange that I was being escorted downstairs, but we were talking, and she had me preoccupied and the thought was fleeting. When we got downstairs and turned the corner to face the aforementioned group of all these people from my life, with my husband right there in front, I was completely confused. He was wearing his, "I wear pink for my wife" t-shirt and there was a lot of other pink in the crowd. Then I was approached by women handing me flowers and a balloon bouquet with a huge pink ribbon floating overhead. I was also handed a giant sign that said, "I'm a Super Survivor". It was like one of those oversized checks that are presented to lottery winners. The whole time, a woman was taking pictures. It was overwhelming and brought me instantly to tears. I still didn't know what was going on.

I turned to someone and asked, "What is happening?" I'm not sure who I first asked, my husband, I think, the beginning of it all was a pink blur behind my tears. My big concern was if my mascara was running since there were all these pictures being taken. I also wished I had put on a little lipstick after lunch and couldn't believe this was happening on one of the few days that I hadn't worn any pink. I usually always wear at least my pink ribbon pin. Once those thoughts cleared and a hundred more pictures were taken, I finally got an answer as to what was taking place.

The hospital representatives explained about the nomination and then let me in on the benefits. I, along with the other two women who were chosen, will go shopping for a new outfit, complete from head to toe. We will each have a visit to a local, high-quality salon for hairstyling including cut and/or color and manicures. The day of the women's fair, we will visit the salon again to have our hair and makeup done. We will then be presented during the fair looking fabulous in our new outfits and makeover. There may be other gifts, as well. Wow! How great is that?

After everyone dispersed and I went back up to the office, there were brownies to top it off. I was caught off guard by all of it. The only other time that I have been so completely surprised, was with my marriage proposal. The difference is that there were only two of us then and there wasn't a photographer capturing my tears and open-mouthed awe. I can sum up how I felt today with a quote from one of my most favorite movies, *Christmas Vacation*; "If I woke up tomorrow with my head sewn to the carpet, I wouldn't be more surprised than I am right now." It was fun! I feel honored, not only for the recognition and the gifts to come but for the onslaught of love and support from all the wonderful people in my life. I have the world's most amazing family, as well as the best friends you could ask for. I'm also fortunate to have a second family at work who has been in this right along with me and has been incredibly supportive and accommodating during all phases of my treatment. I am a woman truly blessed!

That October, I and two other amazing women were honored as Super Survivors during Memorial Medical Center's Women's Health Fair, which coincided with the Making Strides Against Breast Cancer walk. The hospital chooses three breast cancer survivors to highlight and honor during this event each year.

When I was ambushed at work with the announcement, I had no idea what I was in for, but it was an all-around wonderful experience. The three of us ladies had a photoshoot ahead of the event for advertising purposes, which was a nice way to meet and get acquainted. Closer to the health fair, we joined up with the event team to shop for our new outfits. I was mildly chastised when they found out that I had shopped ahead of time and put some items on hold. I couldn't help myself. It takes me forever to find something that I am satisfied with when shopping and knew they wouldn't want to spend three hours with me trying on clothes. I did try on some other options while we were there but ended up with the outfit that I had pre-determined. At least one of the other women admitted to stopping into the store to look around ahead of time, too, but she hadn't gone as far as setting anything aside as I had. We were treated to complete outfits including shoes and jewelry. A few days later, we were sent in for manicures and hair appointments.

The morning of the event, we were chauffeured to the beauty salon for full hair and makeup and changed into our fabulous new ensembles. We were then ushered into the women's fair to have our stories and nominations shared before presenting us on stage before a group of family, friends, and fair attendees. I believe their purpose in highlighting survivors is both to pamper some ladies who have been through a trying, life-threatening situation and to put a face on what it looks like to go through such a thing and come out on the other side as inspiration to others. It was truly an honor to be a face of triumph over adversity and to share it with the people who made that possible. The audience that day included my parents, both of my boys, my husband, my in-laws, three of my cousins, and one aunt. A picture of me with this awesome group of humans, who were all wearing pink and/or pink ribbon shirts, sits on my desk at work. I see it every day and it makes me smile. One picture embodies complete love and includes most of the people I hold most dear in my heart; the same people who formed the foundation of my support system.

August 8, 2015

As I get into bed tonight, I am reflecting on this. Technically, it is now the next day, but it was one year ago that I had my first surgery, August 7, 2014. That morning, when I got up, I was fully intact as God had created me. A mere few hours later, I was minus two breasts and a cancerous tumor that had designs on and was heading for, my lymph nodes. I remember feeling a little nervous that morning, but overall, I was just ready to charge forward and complete what needed to be done. I was joking with the tech when I got my nuclear-med injection and talking with the nurses as I settled into the operating room. I wasn't scared; it was a good morning. I am thankful for that morning; it is why I'm here and in the position that I am a year later. It was a morning of liberation that has allowed me to continue with life free of a disease whose intention was to kill me. Since the growing cancer was fully removed with surgery, I was effectively cancer-free that day.

With that, I feel like I can say that I am now a one-year

cancer survivor. I have passed the first significant mile marker along this road. One down, four to go to reach the all-important five-year mark; that's the one that you strive for. That's the one that statistics are made of. If you can make it those first five years without a recurrence, then the odds are favorable that you will remain free of it. I have a bit of an issue with measuring my life in five-year increments, though. That's what you see when you look at the statistics. It's about who is still alive five, ten, fifteen years later. I want to celebrate every year of my life, but not be surprised that I'm still alive. I want to be able to go back to living like I was before the "big C" came along, but I guess that may not be possible. It will always be there in the back of my mind. I will always approach August 7th with appreciation that I am still here and will keep track, adding to that number each year.

Whether I want to look at it that way or not, I think that I will. That's part of life after cancer. It's the new normal that you fall into line with. I am one of those numbers now; one of the 1 in 8 women who gets breast cancer, one of those who survive the first years and I intend to be among the numbers in the various five-year increments for a long time to come.

PART

III

On with the Show!

MORE THAN A BOOB JOB

August 25, 2015

I know that many have been wondering about this, so it's time to talk about the reconstruction. I want to start by saying that breast reconstruction after cancer is not "just a boob job". I hadn't thought that maybe that's how people see it until I was talking to a fellow member of this tata sisterhood. She had recently had her mastectomy and was just beginning the road to reconstruction while I was recovering from my surgery.

In our conversation, I expressed that things felt different during my second recovery, it felt somewhat lonely. Her response was that was because people see it as "just a boob job". Is that true? Is that how it is perceived? That would fall in line with what I was feeling. It didn't seem to have the same importance or be taken as seriously. I get it; mastectomy surgery is scary and extreme and in response to a life-threatening situation. Reconstruction, however, is not always smooth and no less important for those who choose to undertake it.

This "boob job", is an integral part of repairing the damage that can result from a breast cancer diagnosis. It's putting back a piece of womanhood that was taken away by disease. It is part of cancer treatment. People make light of it, as I have done myself, and say it is the silver lining or bonus for going through all that you go through before getting to this point. In some ways it is. I have joked about it, talked about getting a second job at Hooters, and wondered if I would need a new wardrobe to accommodate a larger bust. Looking at it that way is part of how I have coped with my circumstances. Who wouldn't be excited about the prospect of gaining a cup size or two? But there is more to it than that and it's not quite so simple. And, no, I didn't have to buy a new wardrobe, nor have I applied for that restaurant job.

When this all started, it seemed straightforward enough. The plan was to have a mastectomy, spend a couple of months filling the expanders to stretch the skin, then simply exchange those with implants. That would have been about an hour and a half of surgery, with a week and a half recovery and then back to my regular life. The expectation was for natural-looking breasts a bit bigger than I started with. Things didn't go quite as planned. The unexpected need for chemotherapy delayed the surgery and I ended up with the expanders for nine months. The unwillingness of my body to cooperate and stretch the skin and muscle to well accommodate implants meant a change in surgery plan. Instead, it was a four-hour operation requiring cutting and repositioning of back muscle, moving skin, building up the breasts, as well as, inserting implants and an extra week of recovery. The results of which are breasts that are not quite normal in appearance, loss of sensation in my back and under my arms and a tight stretching, rubber band kind of feeling across my back and chest, that I am told will get better, but never quite go away. I can now easily go without a bra, but the tightness and pulling make it feel as if I'm wearing one even when I'm not. Because of the loss of most of my breast skin and the failure of what was left to stretch and grow, there is not a normal fullness to the under portion. The rest is also tight. They don't jiggle, they don't move. I went jogging braless and it was not even a problem. The natural upside to that is that they will never sag. They do look good in a bra, though, and even without one when covered by clothing.

I am still adjusting to the relocation of part of the lat muscles from my back to my front. I have been working out recently and a couple of the exercises focus on the lats. Since these muscles are now located both in front and back, I feel them being worked in both my mid-back and chest, which is a little weird. On a side note, I have recently discovered that I can control these muscles and can make my chest "dance", as my husband likes to do with his. I have been known to entertain myself this way. It doesn't take much to tickle me.

The patches of skin that were taken from my back and used to add area to my breasts were cut like the profile of a football or an almond eye shape. That is the shape of my scars on each side and something that I am having a hard time getting used to. These are right in front. Once the nipples are added to the middle of this area, I fear they are going to look like eyeballs on my chest. I'm toying with the idea of going all the way with it and just having eyelashes tattooed around the outside of the scars to complete the effect. I won't go that far, but I can't guarantee that I won't draw lashes on just to see what it looks like. I'm teasing about it, but this is the part that I'm most self-conscious about.

I want things to look normal, but they don't, and they never will. It's not as if I'm planning any nude modeling or intend to expose myself to the masses, but I need to be okay with what I see. I also need my husband to be able to look at me as whole again. I find myself keeping mostly covered around him these days. I know I don't need to, and he's never made me feel like I had to, it's just my own insecurity. I am thankful for what I have been given back, even if it will take more time for me to be completely comfortable with it.

I had a great surgical experience and healed quickly without complication. That is not always how it goes. In reading up on reconstruction, I became familiar with a survivor who took four years to complete her reconstruction. She ended up having several surgeries, multiple sets of implants placed, removed, and replaced, had a blood clot and infection. That is just one of many stories of what can go wrong in reconstruction. I am very appreciative of my medical care.

The final procedure to complete my rebuilding will be nipple replacement. As previously mentioned, I have decided to have them tattooed rather than rebuilt. At this point, I don't see a point in actually adding a point.

These will be the cherries on top, so to speak. I am hopeful that this will complete the puzzle and bring it all together. Providing I can get past feeling like my hills have eyes, I think I will see myself as whole again. Nipple reconstruction usually also requires tattooing to add the areola and the color; however, 3D tattooing to complete the whole area instead of reconstructing is gaining popularity. That is what I will have done. I'm taking this final step very seriously. Being careless now could destroy the hope of getting a near-normal final result. I have put much thought and research into my decision.

You may wonder how one would investigate such a thing. In this computer age, it's quite easy, it just required looking at a lot of before and after samples. Those samples, of course, were of women's breasts. I came home from a follow-up appointment with my plastic surgeon and began to fully delve into my choices. At one point, my computer screen was filled with nothing but boobs. My oldest son, who is nineteen, was sitting on the opposite end of the couch as me. He glanced over and did a double take at my computer. He just blurted out, "MOM! What are you looking at?" I could only laugh as I explained. He was quick to point out how he would have been in trouble if the tables were turned, and I found that on his screen. It was quite funny.

I looked at the local option and the nearest other in-state option and didn't feel that either would work for me. In my reading, I discovered that in some places around the country surgeons do the tattooing. They have a small amount of training in this procedure and are, likely, just concerned about adding color and not as much about making them look real. This final step doesn't always seem to be given the importance that I feel it requires. For me, the tattoos need to look as 3D and as real as possible. I want the best for this final procedure, and I have found that at Little Vinnie's Tattoos in Finksburg, Maryland, just outside of Baltimore.

I have decided to travel to Maryland to complete this final step. It is a twelve-hour trip both ways, more than 1500 miles, that will be done in little more than a long weekend. There will be travel expenses and the procedure, which is a bit costly, but barely more than the cost of the other, less acceptable options. How much of it will be covered by insurance remains to be seen. This is an area where, I hear, that most have to fight somewhat with their insurance carrier for even minimal coverage because it is always out of network when done by a tattooist.

Why would I travel so far in such a short time? Because that is where Vinnie Myers has assembled a team who does nipple/areola tattooing for breast cancer patients and they are the best. To look at the pictures on the website, you would never guess that you are only seeing images created with ink and needles. They look like you could reach out and pinch them. There are color variations that add height and depth in places to create the natural-looking bumps and features of an areola. It is true art in a most powerful form.

I have chosen Paul to be my transformist and one conversation with him proved that I had chosen wisely. Not only is he an amazing tattooist/artist, but he is a genuinely nice person. Uncle Pauly, as he is affectionately referred to, could not have been kinder during our phone calls. The questions that he asked about my surgery showed that he is knowledgeable about the different procedures, and he was completely respectful to what I have been through. I have no doubt that he is the right man for this job.

I am excited about the trip and the experience. I have read several articles about this shop and the artists. Breast cancer survivors come from all over the world to be completed by Vinnie's team; many of them are older. One of the articles mentioned the dynamic of a grandma waiting for her reconstruction tattoos sitting next to a biker type in for a traditional tattoo. It's an eclectic mix and will make for a fun way to close out this part of the journey. I have an appointment in October. I will have completed my Herceptin treatments by then and figured Breast Cancer Awareness Month would be a great time to close this chapter. I should feel complete once I have my tattoos. It is odd not having nipples. That is a strange sentence to say, but it's been a strange year.

September 18, 2015

So, this happened today, MY FINAL TREATMENT!!

That was the day of my final Herceptin treatment, signifying the completion of a year of infusions. I wore my sparkly pink shoes and Eric made me an awesome sign referencing one of his favorite movie franchises; it said, "Friday the 18th, the Final Treatment". During the infusion, one of the amazing nurses did as he had done so many times before and asked if he could get me anything. Being the smart alec that I am, I ordered a steak dinner with a baked potato and sour cream. A few minutes later, he came back with a paper copy of said steak dinner. They truly are full-service.

NIP TRIP

October 9, 2015

Today's the big day! I am about an hour from Finksburg, MD, and Little Vinnie's Tattoos. My 3D nipple tattoos are just a couple of hours away. My cousin, Heather, came along as my partner in crime and we drove twelve hours over two days to be here now. I have dubbed this Nip Trip 2015, the ultimate girls' trip for my girls. I felt this was an appropriate and fun way to go about this leg of the journey. Having my cousin by my side makes this that much more special. We have had a great time on our road trip so far. I am so excited to get to Vinnie's! I will go in with a chest that is as blank as the stare of a teenager asked to read a map and come out looking more like I did fourteen months ago before my nipples went off to wherever the organic medical scrap ends up.

I hadn't thought about it too deeply, but I really would like to know how they dispose of that stuff. Those were part of my body and I wonder about their fate. I think I'll have to look into that. At any rate, I'm anxious for my modification. I've gotten so used to seeing myself without nipples that it might take some adjustment to having them again. It is an odd situation to even have to deal with. This is something that the average woman doesn't have to consider but with statistics of one in eight women facing breast cancer, anyone could end up in this scenario.

I have realized that this morning is my final opportunity to test a question that I have had. Could I go out in public topless and not get in trouble for it? I would be a topless woman but without the oh-so offending nipples. It seems to be that a woman can publicly expose every part of her chest as long as the nipples are covered. That is what the attention-monger celebrities do (let us not forget Janet Jackson's famous Superbowl nipple scandal), but I have one up on them since I don't have any to cover up. I have had this discussion with my family and my boys have begged me not to test my theory. I'm several states away, though, so they wouldn't even know unless I got arrested. I hate to pass on this once in a lifetime, limited opportunity but I suppose that I will continue to wonder if I could get away with it. I don't necessarily have a desire to go topless publicly, but the situation is something that I have pondered a bit since this all started. I think I might tell my boys that I did, though, just to see the fear in their teenage eyes. Have to grab those satisfying mom moments when I can. Now, off to get tatted up!

I was both excited and slightly apprehensive as we pulled up to the unassuming tattoo shop in a small strip mall on the side of Highway 140 outside of Baltimore. I had talked to Paul several times and felt completely comfortable with him, I already had one tattoo and had been through that experience but still didn't quite know what to expect.

When we entered the shop, I immediately noticed a map filled with pushpins representing the locations of pink survivors who had added a stop at Little Vinnie's to their personal journey's roadmap. What surprised me most was that there were pins marking locations not just in the states but all around the globe. I was joining a worldwide group adorned with the magical ink that flows through the tattoo guns in the incredibly talented hands of the artists in this local shop. I was honored to add my pin.

Because I mentioned it again in this post, I will add that, to this day, one of the biggest regrets of my whole journey is not having gone outside topless when I believe I could have legally gotten away with it. That was a missed opportunity I will never get back.

Later that night

Wow, it has been quite a day! Driving to the tattoo shop this morning, I started feeling a little emotional thinking of what was about to happen. It was fifteen months ago, exactly, that I was diagnosed, and I haven't felt anywhere near normal since that day. For the month between the diagnosis and my mastectomy, I felt defective, knowing that there was cancer in my body. In the fourteen months since my surgery, I have gone from feeling deformed to adequate, but just not quite complete. I have a good result from my reconstruction, but the final pieces were missing. Tonight, I go to bed feeling like a whole woman again. I'm going to flat out say that my nipples/areolas are amazing! The entire experience was amazing! When I see myself in the mirror now, I feel like pre-cancer me. Having those areas back, makes everything look so different. The scars are not as noticeable and the little imperfections with my reconstructed breasts have faded to the background. I feel more comfortable with the complete look. I am more accepting of myself. I feel great! It's comforting just knowing that they are there. I can't fully explain it, but it is awesome!

I have a very thankful heart tonight! So many people are a part of getting me to this moment. I have to thank my husband for supporting my decision and not telling me that I was crazy when I announced to him that I wanted to drive nearly 800 miles away to a tattoo shop for my nipples. Actually, I didn't tell him that I wanted to, but that I needed to. When he saw the artwork that I was going for, he understood. Eric has loved me through all stages of this journey, and I know that he would have been accepting no matter how I had chosen to complete things, but he understood that I needed to do it this way.

Enormous thanks also go to my cousin, Heather. She happily signed on to be the Louise to my Thelma during this long, but quick trip. Not everyone would make themself available for a four-day trip covering a total of about 1600 miles with 24 hours of riding in the car. That is a lot of love and support. I knew she was the one that I needed here with me from the moment that I decided to make the trip. Having girl time with lots of gabbing and tons of laughs has been a wonderful byproduct. Having her there for this final step was so special. She also served as my personal photographer and got some great pictures to chronicle the entire event. True friends often come in the form of family.

Big props and thanks go to my tattooist, Paul. Uncle Pauly is the man! He is humble about what he does, but I hope he realizes how much he is changing lives. Paul helped to make the whole experience a good one. He was completely respectful, laid back, accommodating, friendly, and put me totally at ease. It goes without saying, but he is a true artist. Incredible talent lives in the man behind the beard and escapes through his tattoo machine. He has left his mark on me, and I couldn't be happier!

Finally, I am grateful for the support that I continue to receive from all of you around me. So many people helped me with the fundraising and just by being there with continued words of encouragement; family, friends, work colleagues, and contacts who I haven't even met in person. I am surrounded by wonderful people who keep me pressing on. Thank you to all of you!

Knowing that we were going to be in the car traveling most daytime hours for the next two days after the tattoos, Paul suggested that I air them out as much as possible when we were in the hotel. How do you know that someone is a true friend? When they don't bat an eye at you hanging around topless while trying to act like you aren't. This is something that we have laughed about since, and I have chuckled about to myself over and over again when revisiting the thought. I have apologized profusely to Heather about her having to deal with my chest being out while getting ready in the morning and watching tv in the room before bed for two days. She was pretty great about it. As family, she and I have been through a lot together, but that was probably close to crossing a line.

Heather is a trouper. She was in the car with me in the winter when I slid through a stop sign and almost went off the road. I was 16 and she was a few years younger. I had been in an accident the previous summer that totaled my car. It had been mostly my fault due to inexperience, panic, and an abruptly stopping driver two cars ahead. I swore her to silence over the icy mishap knowing that family would lose faith in my driving otherwise. That would have been crushing to teenage me after the humiliation of my crash. I don't know if she told anyone, but I never heard about it, so I'm thinking not. I'm spilling it now, but I've driven for an additional 35 years without a major incident and don't care at this point what anyone thinks about my motoring ability. She was also my Maid of Honor on the second go-round and was the one who climbed up under my dress to attempt to fix the train when it came detached and we were short on time. That simple statement doesn't fully express the situation. I can't adequately explain it, but hilarity ensued.

Earlier, I mentioned that Heather was the Louise to my Thelma, but I realize as I think about it, she's more the Ethel to my Lucy. Call yourself fortunate if you have any such person in your life. I am doubly blessed because I have two and both are cousins; the sisters I never had. My other Louise/Ethel is Kim. With our closeness in age and the sheer amount of time that we spent together growing up, she was my first and closest friend. Our shared high jinks would fill a book on their own, but there are still things that neither of us is ready to reveal to our families, so that book will wait. She and I have laughed a million laughs and cried a thousand tears together and possibly evaded jail time. Well, maybe not jail time, it was all just innocent teenage antics, tomfoolery, merrymaking, and shenanigans, except for the underage driving, trespassing, yard signs.... never mind! (Don't tell our kids!) She was my first Maid of Honor who stayed up late with me the night before the wedding to finish flowers that should have long been done. When thinking about the people who formed the backbone of my support system, these two ladies are right there as an important part of what held me together then as they had before and still do to this day. My cousins, my sisters; my sister-cousins. No, that's not right, that's a bad reality show. Part of my family is from Kentucky, but not the backwoods. Let's just leave it at two of my favorite humans.

November 4, 2015

I could not be more pleased with my results, they are amazing! I have shown pictures of my tattoos to many, and the reaction is always sheer surprise at the realism. My husband fears that I have become an exhibitionist. Do you remember the John Candy movie, *Summer Rental*, and the neighbor? She had gotten a boob job and was showing everyone, whether they wanted to see or not. I'm not that bad and so far, have only shown pictures and never by force. I want to spread the word about this wonderful option for nipple replacement. It was a super experience! The atmosphere was very professional and respectful, laid back, and comfortable. This team has it together and is helping so many women complete this journey. I am fully thankful that this exists and grateful to Paul for blessing me with his artwork and helping me to feel whole again.

I will take every opportunity to put out information for those who may not be familiar with this amazing, non-invasive option that affords realism without a surgical procedure and bypassing a bra if you so choose. What woman wouldn't choose that if she could? I am extremely grateful for the gentleman who did my reconstructive nipple tattoos. That's exactly what he is, too, a gentleman. Some hold the misconception that having this done in a tattoo shop somehow makes it inappropriate. On the contrary, it was every bit safe, sanitary, private, and respectful. What it wasn't, was stiff and clinical. Paul seems able to adapt well to his client's personality, so in my case, there was plenty of joking and laughter, which made it an easier process.

When I was preparing for my trip, some didn't quite understand what I was doing. Some thought I was getting tattoos over my scars of maybe flowers or something. I know women who have had that done and they end up wearing really beautiful pieces of art. I wasn't wanting to cover my scars, but rather complement them and return my breasts to a more natural landscape. My scars represent my journey. They no longer bother me, instead, I see them as part of this new, healed, stronger me. I appreciate them. They live with me, and I live because of them. So, rather than getting flowers or butterflies, I got tattoos of nipples, very realistic replicas that just happened to be placed in the area where my original ones used to live.

Thinking of it that way harkens back to a previous bemusing. These are just tattoos, so if they were placed anywhere else on my body, I could expose them, show pictures of them, have them out in public, but, because of their placement, they become private. Kind of an interesting thought to twirl around. I guess I'm still trying to decide if I could legally go topless because I don't have nipples, but
rather pictures of them in less than coincidental places. Perhaps I do have a little exhibitionist in my blood.

I have spoken of this a lot to help people understand that it isn't just coloring in the area of the areola. That is something that can be done by cosmetic tattooists and even some surgeons and serves mostly to provide color to reconstruction. In the case of it being done by surgeons, it seems like most are likely to draw a small circle inside a larger circle and color it in with either a shade of pink or a shade of brown, depending on skin tone. In my case, it is having the appearance of the nipple-areola area created to look 3D with nothing more than a tattoo needle, an array of ink, and artistic talent.

As Paul was setting up his supplies, Heather and I were shocked at the array of ink colors that were being put out. I think we both expected to see pink and brown, but were shocked by the teal, purple, yellow, green, red, black, and peach. Those were used to mix the different shades needed to match my skin tone and the coloring of the previous inhabitants to match them as closely as possible. One more surprising aspect that goes into putting it all back together.

I can barely express how much having this done has helped me to finish healing and feel whole and complete again. I feel sexy and more like myself now. I was finally able to remove my shirt in front of my husband again, even with the lights on, without feeling self-conscious. When I see my nude self, I feel good about it, I'm not slammed with a reminder of where I've been the last year and a half. That's the result of a good reconstruction result paired with superior tattoo completion. I admit that I have spent quite a bit of time examining them in the mirror, still in disbelief. The degree of realism that has been achieved on my chest cannot be done by just anyone or even just any tattooist. I encourage this option for breast patients in need but do your research before signing up. Many claim to be at this level, but few truly are. There are a few others out there, but if you end up at Little Vinnie's, tell them I sent you.

When tattooing was concluded, I turned to the full-length mirror to face my new self for the first time and was instantly overwhelmed with tears of joy. I was shocked and amazed that I had so quickly been returned to a complete version of myself. This finishing touch was a powerful piece of my recovery and renewal.

Here's a quick story to close and attest to the realism of these mere tattoos: As I was waiting to be taken down to the operating room to have my chemo port removed, I realized that my chest was going to be exposed. I thought I better give the nurses a little heads up so they wouldn't be confused by what they were going to see. As a couple of them were wheeling me to the operating room, I decided to clue them in. Keep in mind, I had already had a little shot of happy juice in my IV. I said that I wanted to warn them that when they saw my chest, they might be surprised because I have only tattoos in place of nipples. They said that they had seen that before, no big deal, but I told them that I didn't think they had probably seen ones like mine. I added that I had traveled to Maryland to have them done. When I came to in recovery, one of the same nurses was there with me. She looked at me with big eyes and agreed that I was right. She said that mine were the best they had ever seen. Well, thank you!

TAKING CARE OF
(someone else's) BUSINESS

November 20, 2015

My teenage son has been sick, really sick. He has been set up on the couch where I spent my recovery time and in much the same way. It's covered with the same *Pirates of the Caribbean* sheet, he has multiple blankets and pillows, the phone, his computer, there are ice packs and towels and medicine sitting around. It's a familiar arrangement, a familiar sight. When I was there, he spent so many days at the other end of that couch just sitting with me and being there in case I needed anything. Lately, I have been in there with him whenever I can for the same reasons, even sleeping on another small couch when he was up several times in the night. For about two and a half weeks now, he hasn't been able to keep anything down. I won't give the details, but they are quite unpleasant. He is miserable and has lost a lot of weight. He's uncomfortable, has been in pain, has had trouble sleeping, and is scared. We have seen five doctors, been to the ER, and had multiple tests with no answers and little relief. We are still working on it and hoping for a resolution soon.

Here's the purpose in me bringing this up; he told me that he now knows how I felt when I was living on the couch during my recoveries. He brought up the night that I had my breakdown and just started crying. At that point, I was frustrated, tired of being confined to the couch, but I had a hard time getting up and moving around and couldn't sleep in the bed. I was in pain and felt awful. I was tired of the living room, tired of lying there, tired of watching tv, but didn't feel like reading or getting on the computer. I hated having to ask for things from others and feeling like a burden; I was getting depressed. He had reached the same point of being tired of just lying there, but not having the strength or want to do anything else, of being sick of the tv, but not wanting to use the computer, of feeling like a burden and not wishing to bother someone else with things for him, fed up with being ill and the resulting issues. Roles had reversed. I am now on the other side of it as the caregiver in a frightening situation. There have been two other times with my kids that have been similarly scary, but this is the first time I have felt so helpless. This is a reminder to me of what it feels like to be in this spot and of what my husband went through as my caregiver during my surgeries and cancer treatment. It has served as an example of what he may have been feeling as the one on this side without the answers or any way to immediately make things better.

When someone has a debilitating illness, injury, or disease, you feel sympathy and empathy for that person, but how much do you think about the person or people who are taking care of them? It's hard on the patient, for sure, but, at a point, they settle into whatever is happening and go with it. The person on the outside providing care is in a constant state of alert and action and concern. There is, also, the matter of the time and energy that it requires to administer that care and the things that have to be put on hold or rearranged. There is time spent waiting at appointments and trips to the store for medication and supplies. There may be difficult or unpleasant aspects of care or cleaning things up that have to be done. Sometimes, what is needed is just for you to provide company or levity, to hold a hand, stroke a forehead or just be present in the room.

In addition to the physical aspect is the mental anguish that the one giving care can experience; the constant worry, the want to make it better without any way to do that, the guilt of feeling that you aren't doing enough or can't be there all the time, the fear of the unknown in it all and fear that things may not ever go back to normal. I know that there are times when it is harder on the attendant than the patient. Not everyone can be that caregiver, not everyone has that in them and that's okay, but when you have been the patient and had that person who was there for you, you appreciate it in a deep and lasting way. I am grateful to my caregiver. My husband, who had only held that title for nine months before my diagnosis, got the job by default, but he showed up in a big way. He was there by my side the entire time. Whatever was needed, he did it. He was there to help me get up. Sounds simple, but that can be a difficult task when you have to be careful of surgical areas and the patient can't push or pull with their arms; there's a lot of scooting and maneuvering and caution on the side of the helper. Getting back down into position can be just as much a struggle. When ice was a part of recovery, he filled ice bags and fetched ice packs constantly. He got me drinks, fixed my food, changed bandages, emptied, and cleaned surgical drains, bathed me, and even washed my hair. He made countless trips to the store for medication, supplies, and any other need or want. He sat with me and held my hand, he made me laugh, he kissed my forehead, he sometimes fielded frustration and held me when I cried, not knowing what else to do. He was there for me for every little thing.

We had a morning routine and a bedtime routine. Before he went to work, he would get me up and help me clean up. The first step was emptying drains and measuring and recording the volume of fluid in them. With my second surgery, I had four drains to care for instead of just two. Next, he would gently wash me and help me get into clean clothes. The exception, here, would be some days when my mom took washing and dressing duty. When I was at the point that I could do those things for myself, he would wait outside the bathroom in case I had a need. After that, he would see if I wanted any breakfast and then get me settled back on the couch with fresh ice packs and make sure that I had my medicine and a drink and anything else I would require for the day. If the cat wasn't already there, he would bring her to me, as well. Then he drove carpool to school and went off to work, knowing that there would be more to do when he got home.

After work, there were trips to the store, preparing meals and changing ice packs. Time was spent just hanging out, watching tv or movies and talking about the day before the bedtime routine started. Before going off to bed, he took care of my needs, which included, checking, and emptying the drains again, changing clothes and cleaning up, getting medication or anything else, and settling me into position for the night, adding the cat to the equation, and changing out ice packs. So many ice packs! We had our routines down.

I know it all wore on him, it would have to, but he never showed that to me. He never made me feel like a burden. I know that he worried about me. I think there were probably thoughts about the unknown of recovery and some of the treatment. I realize, in the beginning, there were questions of what the future would hold or if I would even have a future. That's natural, but I tried to quash those thoughts right away. I don't know if he had little breakdowns if he had to count to ten and take a breath or wished that life had taken a different turn. I wouldn't blame him if he did, but he would never tell me. All that I saw was love, concern, and support.

I am aware that my experience with cancer treatment would have been very different had it happened when I was on my own with my kids; it would have been immensely harder. I would have required more outside help and would have been more alone on occasion. Timing is truly everything! I was fortunate to not only have my husband to care for me but also my mother and my two boys to help out. My kids were fourteen and eighteen at the time of my diagnosis. They did what they could for me. They never passed by without asking if I needed something. They fetched drinks and took their turns with the ever-present ice packs, among other things. Sometimes they were just there, to talk or sit with me. I know it was hard on them, too. In their cases, once the fear of my possible death passed, the most difficult part was probably seeing the woman that they knew to be strong and indestructible in pain, vulnerable, and needing help. It was a year that changed all of us.

I was thinking about my point in writing this and I have more than one. It's not just to say that I am a blessed woman but it's to say that you never know what curveball life is going to throw you. There are times that we all need help, even stubborn, independent women who will exhaust all avenues before asking for it. When those times arrive, some are going to surprise themselves with the aid that they are able to provide. We are often able to endure much more than we ever knew we were capable of no matter which side of a situation we fall on.

Whichever side you land on, consider what the person on the reverse could be feeling. The person being cared for is appreciative of all that is being done, likely feels bad that they require so much assistance, and hates that they may be putting someone out. They don't want to be a burden and would much rather be able to take care of things for themself. The person providing care is doing it, not just out of necessity, but out of love. They don't see you as a burden, and even though they may be tired or stressed, they will do whatever is needed. They want only for things to get better. The struggle is in accepting the other person's position and reconciling your own.

This seems like a good place for a random thought. A couple of years ago, I was walking around the neighborhood. I tend to kind of glance at windows as I walk along and see what there is to see. I'm not a Peeping Tom or Tina, I'm just curious about how other people's houses are set up and decorated. Anyway, I passed a house with a large picture window in the front and noticed a hospital bed set up near it. I wondered what the situation was. At that moment, it was driven home to me that you never know what is going on in someone else's life. When you encounter people throughout the day, you don't know what struggles they may be coping with. You don't know if they are dealing with an illness or a loss or if they are caring for someone in a difficult situation. We need to have compassion for our fellow humans. We need to be available to those who require help and to thank the ones who provide it. Never let an opportunity pass to appreciate a connection in your life.

So far, this tale has been my outlook on how the pink disease affected me with only a slight nod to what may have been taking place with others. That makes sense since this is the story of my experience, but there is also a story in how such a thing affects the loved ones of the diagnosed. I wanted to share a bit of that, so I turned to a co-worker whose mother is also a breast cancer survivor. I knew he could give the son's perspective that I needed without having to ask my kids. I felt like they may not open up fully to me for fear that it would be too much for each of us. Thank you to my friend for graciously exposing his feelings on this personal matter. He has provided an honest and heartfelt look into the mind of a son facing an unexpected fear.

I have come to know Kellby in the past couple of years and he and I have shared many laughs and interesting stories. One day, as he was standing at my desk noticing the array of pink ribbon-laden pictures and sayings posted around it, we had a conversation about my breast cancer status. He then shared with me that his mother is also a survivor. That kind of interaction is one of the reasons that I am so open about my own experiences; it creates an avenue for connection and conversation that may be needed and not readily available. It is comforting to be aware of the difficult things you have in common with others, so you know you are not alone in those situations. The additional reason that I'm so open is that I like to talk and tend to have few boundaries. Can you say, TMI? I can, but rarely do.

At 23, Kellby was living in Arizona, several states away from his parents in Illinois. He was working for an airline teaching a class, Emergency Preparedness and Response to Aircraft Incidents. At that point, he had been away from home since signing up with

Uncle Sam at the tender age of 18 and giving four years to the Marine Corps. He turned 19 in boot camp and 21 during a tour in Afghanistan. What he was about to face would test him as much as anything he encountered during that time.

Kellby's mom called one day while he was teaching class. He ignored the call, intending to get back to her later. When she quickly called a second time, he knew that it must be important, so he gave the class a break and returned the call. His mother answered crying. She took a breath and simply said, "I have breast cancer." At that moment, his military training kicked in and he questioned what the next step was and what all needed to be done. She didn't have much information at the time, it was all very new. He asked what he could then they ended the call, that's when his tears came. He felt helpless knowing he couldn't do anything for her from such a distance.

There was no way he could continue right then, so the class was excused for an hour meal break; they were co-workers and understood. He went to lunch with his boss and a friend, needing time to pull it together and process what he had just learned. After two bites of food, he promptly threw up in the airport terminal. His flight home was the next day.

During that flight, Kellby says he cycled through the stages of grief as if he had lost a fellow Marine. He was full of rage and angry at everyone and everything. He was mad at God. Why would He allow that to happen to her? He was mad at the doctor. Why didn't he catch it sooner? He was mad at his mom, thinking maybe she could have prevented it if she had taken care of herself differently. He was mad at the Marine Corps for taking him away from her for four years of his life. He was also mad at himself for not being there and not being able to help. Those are common questions and feelings that arise with a diagnosis but are most times unwarranted, and he knew that. It's a quick reaction, a way to try and justify what's happening and place the blame somewhere. When those immediate thoughts settle down, you find your footing and come around to what is going on and work to figure out where you fit into the process.

Her cancer was found to be stage 2 and she had two types, both invasive and non-invasive. He had a passing thought that she might not survive it as they waited for details of the disease and treatment but pushed thought away because she is such a strong woman, he knew that couldn't happen. She would have a lumpectomy, chemo, and radiation. The chemo was the scariest part of all of it for Kellby. He knew how tough it was on her and she would sometimes call him in the middle of the night; because he doesn't sleep much, that wasn't a problem. He and his mom have always had a very strong and close relationship, which made it even harder for him to know she was suffering. It was in those times that he feared she may actually die from the treatment rather than the disease.

Kellby made the observation that dealing with a parent's cancer can be similar to being a young person in the military. It forces you to grow up quickly in the face of a life and death situation, be it aiding wounded troops, squaring off with armed militants, or being at the side of the woman you are closest to in this world as she is sick and hurting. On the surface, you are strong, you step up and man up but at heart, you are still that immature kid making inappropriate jokes in the barracks.

She came through her treatments successfully and has been six years cancer-free. The experience has left an indelible impression on this tough Marine with a big heart. He has a fear of other friends or family going through the same thing but after seeing how his mom handled it, knows it can be defeated. Of more value, though, is his final word on the matter, "You should never sacrifice time with loved ones for your career, the loved ones are always more important." I feel that's good advice. It's my opinion that the love of family and friends is more valuable than any job or the balance in your bank account.

WHAT DOESN'T KILL YOU MAKES YOU STRONGER - AND HOTTER

February 26, 2016

I had lunch last week with another breast cancer survivor who posed an interesting question to me; "Did you ever think that cancer might kill you?" The answer to that is yes and no. I guess the bigger answer is that I try to not think about it in that light if I can help it.

The first time that I considered that I could die from breast cancer, was during a conversation with my husband. It was shortly after I was diagnosed, and he was still trying to process what was going on. We were sitting at the kitchen counter, he looked at me bewildered and asked what would happen to him if something happened to me. There was the question of where he would live. Because I had a big enough house that I had fought to keep, it made sense to live in it after we were married. Being newlyweds, we hadn't gotten everything transferred and his name wasn't on the house, so that was a concern. I knew what he was really thinking was how could he possibly live without me, but, at the time, it was more of where he would live without me. It's funny what comes to mind when faced with big situations like that. I told him that it didn't matter because I wasn't going anywhere, I wasn't going to die.

That did make me think, for a moment, about what would happen. What would happen to the house? What about my boys? Would they automatically end up with their dad? Could my mom possibly take them? Would they have a choice? Should I have maybe acted on making a will before now? Do I have time to clean out my closet and get rid of all my junk in case something does happen, so no one else has to do it? A lot of questions, none that I much wanted to think about.

I had never truly been afraid of breast cancer; I had been

very aware of it, because of the extreme family history, but it didn't scare me. Maybe that was naive, but it was how I felt. I had witnessed five women in my family face it. I had seen that, when treated, it was possible to go on with your life. I watched my mom go through it twice with, what seemed like, relative ease. From my perspective, it looked straightforward and simple, even though I know now that it wasn't quite so. My mom is a very private person who never wants to burden anyone and will do almost anything before asking for help. She is strong and independent. I am thankful to take after her in those areas, but because of those traits, I didn't fully know what she experienced. I now know more of what she dealt with, but what she showed me then shaped the way that I thought about breast cancer and is most of the reason that I didn't fear it.

When she was first diagnosed, I was about to be married. I was young and was selfishly focused on what I was doing and didn't see all that was happening with her. I didn't live at home, but we worked together, so I got a glimpse there. What I witnessed was her going through surgery without complication and continuing to work through radiation. I knew that she had some skin irritation and burning and that she was a bit tired, but she functioned as usual and never complained.

A few years later, when cancer arose on the other side, she did it all again and in the same manner. Fast forward twenty-plus years and she is well and hasn't had another issue related to those cancers. What she showed me was that you could face it, treat it, and go on.

I saw two other aunts successfully treat their cancers and continue on, both well today. It appears that the type of cancer in our family is slow-growing and highly treatable in the early stages. Three strong women were the face of breast cancer for me, and I always saw it as something to address and move on.

The two family members that I watched die from it were different situations. Their diagnoses and treatments came far too late in the game. Those fights stressed to me how important early diagnosis and treatment are. I began my mammograms early; my doctor's exams were thorough, and I was conscious of my breast health. I never feared it. I also didn't know much about it. I figured that, when my time came, I would face it and defeat it just as my mom had. The difference being, I had decided to have a full mastectomy at the first sign of anything, but I expected that to be it. The possibility of an aggressive type of cancer never occurred to me. I didn't realize that there are many types and various grades of breast cancer. Why I didn't do more research into those things prior to joining the family pink club I don't know. I think, in my mind, even though I always knew that I had an increased risk, I hoped that there would be something that would preclude me from walking that path.

The second time that it occurred to me that I could lose my life in this, was in the surgeon's office during my mastectomy follow-up. When he told me that, although the cancer was stage one, small, wasn't in my lymph nodes, and hadn't spread, it was grade three for aggressiveness and that chemo would be involved in treatment, it hit me that it wasn't as simple as I had thought. I had a momentary breakdown, then got my head together and determined to press forward. That is when I started educating myself on the types and treatments of breast cancer. I was encouraged to find that there are highly successful treatments for early-stage, triple-positive disease, as I had. I had total confidence in my medical team and the treatments that were put before me. I questioned everything, as I tend to do, and did my reading on all of it, but I felt good about where it was headed. My fears were allayed.

Now, momentary thoughts arise about the possibility of my life finding conclusion at the end of a pink ribbon, when I hear or read about specific breast cancer deaths. It isn't stories of the deaths of those who had later stage cancer or a type that is harder to treat, who fought a fierce battle from the beginning that get me down deep, it's the ones who thought they had successfully eradicated it, only to have it arise somewhere else as metastatic cancer that truly scare me. It's the sneakiness of those cancers and the aggressive factors that are frightening. I try to push those thoughts out of my head when they roll in, but for a moment, I consider the possibility.

I reassure myself that I have done everything needed to rid my body of cancer and have followed a treatment plan to decrease the likelihood of any recurrence to somewhere below 10%. That being said, parts of that treatment have been linked to causing other cancers. The chemo drugs, the Neulasta shot after each treatment and the Tamoxifen that I took daily for several months all have histories that include bringing about new cancers, unrelated to the breast, in other areas. I know I would be infuriated to end up with a different cancer as a result of getting rid of the original. I considered that prospect when planning treatment and, ultimately, banked on the benefits outweighing the risk.

That is completely out of my hands since we are after the fact, but those occurrences are rare.

That is what I push to the front of my mind when I have thoughts otherwise. I also try to focus on the stories that you don't hear as much about; all of the success stories, the long-term survivors, those who put the experience behind them and go on to live full, complete lives. Stories like my mom's. You don't hear those as often because the story turns into a continuance of life as we know it. What you hear most of are the odd situations, the rare happenings, the details of gallant fights when those fights are lost. Those are at the forefront. They absolutely should be, don't get me wrong, but every story is noteworthy, especially when it is a grand success story. I wish that we heard more stories and statistics about the ones whose breast cancer fight is just a footnote to their life and not the exclamation point. There needs to be more highlighting of long-term survivors, those who are past 20, 30, even 40 years. Statistics focus on numbers based on deaths because they are easier to track, rather, let us focus the numbers on lives. There should also be more talk about those who are living with stage 4, living with it, not dying from it. I recently saw info on some stage 4 survivors who were more than 10 years into maintenance chemo that was allowing them to continue their lives. Those are the things that we need to hear and see, to instill hope and provoke determination.

I have to be of a mindset that I will be in that group where I can look back and barely see my cancer in the past. When I first met with the surgeon who would do my mastectomy, he told me that I was going to be fine and that he didn't see any reason that I shouldn't still be around to be a great-grandmother. That is what I have held on to. I am past the year and a half cancer-free mark at this point. I am healthy, I feel good, my continuing treatment is only one pill a day and I have a head full of hair, I'm in a great place. That should make me feel good, and it does, but sometimes it also makes me feel guilty.

Being in this special club, as I am, I have come to know both survivors and current fighters. When I am hearing about or in the vicinity of ladies who are actively in the fight of their lives, some who are deep in it and those who are losing or have lost it, I think, "There but by the grace of God go I." Why am I where I am when others do all the same things but end up battling just to live another day? It isn't fair and seems so random, like an involuntary lottery that you don't want to win. I shouldn't feel guilty, but rather I am thankful. Thankful for the treatment, for the support, for my continued health, and for the opportunities that I have to shed light on this disease and put a face to it. We are all sisters (and some brothers, too) in this, we represent each other, support each other, cheer successes, and mourn losses.

In the beginning, I felt uneasy about the term "survivor". I felt like it put the focus on the fact that, gee, I was still here, like I shouldn't be or maybe wouldn't have been. Something about that didn't sit right with me. I felt like I wasn't "surviving", I was just living, as I always had. Early on, I talked with a ta-ta sister who had stage 0 cancer. That is the earliest stage, non-invasive, and hasn't spread. There were cancer cells involved, it was cancer. She endured a mastectomy and a complicated reconstructive surgery. She told me that she didn't feel right being called a survivor, because it was at such an early stage and that she hadn't truly fought a fight. We decided that we preferred to be called warriors instead. I think that was wrong, though. I do like the term warrior and have called myself a pink warrior, but I have also since embraced the survivor moniker. We are survivors. Anyone who has had cancer and is still here to talk about it is a survivor. Wear the badge with honor. The survivors put a face on it, add hope to it and highlight the footprints that others have left behind. I feel as though I have found my purpose in this journey, and the purpose is the journey. If my experience can benefit any person, then it has value.

Did I ever think that I might die from my cancer? Once

upon a time, but no longer; instead, I choose to live despite it and richer because of it. I face each day with a new appreciation of the beauty around me and the people beside me, make note of the little things that make it all special, take nothing for granted, and strive to uphold my purpose.

A small footnote is needed here. When I wrote that entry, both of my surviving aunts were healthy, as noted. As I am writing this, the one aunt who is a two-time survivor now has ovarian cancer, which may or may not be related. She is being treated and we are hopeful that things will turn out well. I also lost a friend who ended up with stage 4 breast cancer about 25 years after her initial diagnosis and treatment. She was the one who talked me through my reluctance to complete my chemo plan. She did everything right, but it found her again anyway. This is the underlying fear of every cancer survivor. It's the tiny voice in the recesses of your mind that you hope never speaks up to say, "Hey, remember me? I'm baaack!"

May 31, 2016

I had to laugh when I woke up the other morning. Looking at me and my side of the bed, you would have thought a tornado had come through. My pillow was waded up, the covers were pulled off the bed and pushed into a pile up against my husband and my hair looked like I told my stylist that I wanted a cross between Einstein and Don King. Then, I looked at my other half all nicely covered up with the sheet and comforter smooth over him, head resting flat on the pillow splayed out beneath him with only the hair touching it in back messed up. He may move from his back to side occasionally, but it looks like I participate in MMA bouts on my side of the bed. This is how I wake up every day, but for some reason, I took note of the whole scene that day and it tickled me.

I'm not kidding about the hair thing, it is crazy when I wake up, standing up all over my head. It was worse when it was shorter, but it still gets pretty wild. The reason for this messy state of affairs is that I don't sleep soundly. I haven't slept solidly through a night since this whole thing started, coming up on two years ago. There may have been a few random nights of knocked-out sleep after surgeries when I was heavily medicated, but none beyond that. In the beginning, the reason was worry and a continual thought process that didn't shut down for the night. After surgery and reconstruction began, I lost sleep due to discomfort. The discomfort then mixed with side effects from chemo to continue the restless nights into the next year. Now, my lack of satisfying sleep is mostly attributed to the horrendous hot flashes and occasional night sweats served courtesy of my daily medication.

As part of treatment for hormone-positive breast cancer, daily hormone suppressing medication is suggested to lower estrogen levels, and, thereby, lessen the possibility of the cancer growing or recurring. One of the main side effects of this pill is hot flashes, which can also be paired with night sweats. This is prescribed for five years. I've got just over one down.

I'm pretty sure I made light of it when my mom mentioned hot flashes, so, maybe this is karma. Just like karma, hot flashes are a bitch, with a capital B. When they first started, I thought they were bad, but I had no idea what I was really in for. It's not simply getting a little heated, you feel like your blood is boiling and then you start sweating. I feel it in my face and head first, then it spreads. It's like an atmospheric glimpse into hell itself. After more than a year of this, I'm adjusting, and finding ways to deal. I try to layer my clothes when I can, so I can take one piece off, then put it back on, then take it off, and so on. It's become a joke in my office. I have a fan on my desk that I turn off and on every half hour or so. One minute I'm sweating, the next I'm freezing. That's how it goes. It's worse at night. I start sweating, so I throw the covers off, then I get cold. I get back under the covers all cozy, then start sweating again. Because of the sweat, I'm wet, and then because of being damp, I get cold. Covers on, covers off, covers on, one leg out, both legs out, covers on, covers off, etc. It's a dance I do all night long. The cat gets annoyed by all the movement, and she ends up leaving. I think my husband sleeps through most of it, I'm not sure how much it bothers him.

I know that one night it did wake him, and it was quite funny. On that night, I was greatly struggling. I was sweating like crazy and couldn't take it. I had already gotten up and stripped everything off, but that didn't fix it. I thought that cranking up the ceiling fan, which is just over the end of our bed, would help. Since the chain to adjust the speed is short and I am, too, I had to stand on the bed to reach it. So, the room was dark, it was about 2 am, I was naked standing on the foot of the bed stretching to reach the chain to turn up the fan; I was teetering a little due to being half asleep and balancing on the bed. I started to fall, but caught myself, jostling the bed and waking Eric up. Imagine his surprise to find me hovering naked above him. He didn't know if he was under attack or about to get lucky. I still laugh about that one.

The blood-boiling heat is an annoyance, but a small price to pay for, potentially, life-saving medication. I sleep with loose covers that I can easily manipulate and keep at least one leg out; the ceiling fan is always on a decent speed and, I remind myself, only four more years.

FIXER-UPPER - CHEST EDITION

March 9, 2017

So, I realized that I haven't posted much this year. Time has gotten away from me as I'm mostly going about life as usual. Well, sort of, anyway. My usual will always be different now. Tonight, I'm focused on the morning. Heading in for surgery bright and early.

I'm looking forward to tomorrow as it is something that I had been contemplating and decided that I needed to do to be able to move forward and get back to feeling as comfortable in my skin as possible. I'm having a revision to my reconstruction. I requested it because I haven't been completely happy with the way things settled in and shaped up. My result isn't an issue with a medical procedure or care, it's merely how my body responded to everything and took to its new parts. Just as with remodeling a house, sometimes new additions require a few tweaks and tucks to be right.

I had a successful surgery the first time and healed without any major issues. I had been apprehensive about pursuing additional procedures because I healed so well. I was afraid that I might be tempting fate to go at it again. I have read about and heard horror stories of reconstructions that went terribly wrong. Infections and incisions that don't heal properly can cause enormous problems and require implant removal and more follow-up procedures resulting in additional time spent trying to piece things together and get back to where you were. I finally got over that, though, and decided to head back in and fix things up. I have complete faith and trust in my doctor and the facilities at my disposal. I feel fortunate to have the opportunity to improve my form. It may seem to be merely cosmetic, but, for me, this plays a huge part in healing and dealing with life after cancer. I need to get close to my pre-disease state so I can see only myself in the mirror and not always feel like a victim of the breast stealing, life-sucking BC bandit.

I've been feeling a bit nervous about this surgery but wasn't sure why. I had four surgical procedures within about 16 months when this all started and had very little anxiety about any of them. I determined that is the issue. I haven't had a procedure in almost two years. When this began, I was a surgery virgin, but I wasn't worried the first time. Instead, I was charged up, I was ready, I simply wanted the cancer out. I remember that morning and my attitude was, "Let's do this!" After that, my life became a series of sticks and pokes and cuts and drugs. Sounds like a bad after-school special or something I might need an intervention from. It all began as a whirlwind and I was blowing around from one thing to another not thinking about it, just doing what needed to be done. First was the mastectomy surgery with expander insertion, then surgery to place a port, then chemo every three weeks with blood draws and the follow-up shot the next week, then reconstructive surgery, during which time infusions of Herceptin continued to be administered for a full year, then came surgery to remove the port. That was November of 2015, and the atmosphere has been pretty calm since. I came out the other side of it a bit windblown but have enjoyed the low pressure that has followed. Currently, I merely have blood drawn every six months; but it seems the wind is starting to rotate again, so why not just flip up my collar and head right back into it. Let's get it done!

March 11, 2017

Surgery went well. It'll be another two days before I can unwrap and see what's happening beneath the bandaging. Several things took place in the operating room. Both implants were removed and replaced with a different size and fat was extracted via liposuction from my back and from under my arms where the back scars and movement of the lat muscle around to my chest had trapped it. I'm expecting that to eliminate the bulging areas under my arms that made it feel like I was smuggling rolled up tube socks beneath them. The fat that was taken out was then grafted into my chest to reshape it. That was followed by some tightening and tucking. A small bonus was that the doctor needed a little more fat, so she took that from my belly. I told her to take all she wanted. I'm anxious to see what that's going to look like. I'm hoping my tummy is a tad flatter. That area is the sorest right now. She also fixed my port scar. That silly little scar constantly itched and was irritated when clothes rubbed against it. It had become a hypertrophic scar, meaning it was thick and raised. I'm not doing bad tonight. With pain meds, ice packs, and keeping mostly still, the worst pain is when I have to get up. Looking forward to Sunday when I'll get to shower.

April 2, 2017

Hey, I'm back! I am now three weeks post-surgery. Feeling fairly good, aside from a nasty virus that I'm currently fighting, but that's not in any way related. Some areas are still a bit sore at times but getting better every day. I have had people asking how I'm doing and have had much to say but wasn't able to get it together. While I was on the pain meds, my vision was blurry, and typing was difficult. I was also a bit hazy and tired. I went off the medication to go back to work, but then I was exhausted when I got home. I went back too early, just five days after surgery, and that didn't help with my other issue. That issue would be the depression that I tend to experience after surgery.

I appear to go through a similar cycle each time. I don't feel bad right after but, of course, that is when I'm on a regular schedule of pain medication and sleeping a lot. Then, once I stop the medicine, I get frustrated with the pain and limitations and have a mini breakdown then get depressed. That, thankfully, doesn't last long, because that just isn't me and I don't like being that way. During that time, I didn't feel like writing. I also needed to be sure that I was in the correct frame of mind to not come off whiny and I wanted to get a good view of how things were healing so I could provide a fair assessment.

Surgery morning got underway with me dressed in the lovely purple paper gown hooked up to the warm air blower that I've now become accustomed to. (Say that ten times fast; purple paper gown, purple paper gown, purple paper gown... sorry, that just struck me as funny when I was reading it back) It's quite the fashion statement when it fills up with air. When matched with the hospital surgical cap, it's a classic. I could totally see it on the runways of Paris. Not even kidding, you've seen some of the crazy stuff that passes for fashion in celebrity circles. I've talked previously about this gown and how the warm air keeps you toasty while waiting to go to the operating room. It's quite cozy. Hooked up, lounging in the recliner with the remote to adjust the heat, the tv remote, and another pair of non-skid socks to add to my collection, it almost felt like preparing for a spa visit rather than going to be sliced open. I'm a tad disappointed that I didn't come out with a manicure but, nail polish isn't allowed in the OR. To be serious, though, I looked into this gown. The purpose is to keep your body temperature up to avoid hypothermia after surgery. Anesthesia lowers your temperature, and the operating room is kept quite chilly, too. A lowered body temp can open you up to infection. Nice that they provide these now as added protection and to promote the best healing. It's warm, but also pretty cool.

After the fashion show, my doctor came in to draw on me and map out the plan. You know you have a good relationship with your doctor when it doesn't bother you to stand naked in front of the mirror while she draws on you in blue pen. The tic-tac-toe game on my hip was fun, but her name in graffiti across my belly was a bit much. I am completely kidding, I'm sure she would never do that. Well, not completely sure, but I honestly wouldn't care if she did. Her smiling face always puts me at ease. I feel like it's going to be alright when she enters the room. Her cheer coupled with the professionalism of all the staff helped me take that familiar walk to the operating room with confidence.

Headed for surgery without worry.

The operation seems to have gone as planned, at least I didn't hear otherwise. The last thing I remember, I was being assisted onto the table and placed face down. The first part of the procedure was to be lipo on my back, so I started out lying on my belly. The anesthesiologist was telling me that she was going to give me just a little....and, I was gone. I woke up in recovery groggy with a dry mouth and scratchy throat. At that point, I was in quite a bit of pain, so I got a little shot of morphine in my IV, ate a couple of Lorna Dune cookies, the go-to at the clinic, with a little soda, and came around enough to get dressed and out of there.

It's a strange feeling to have a period of time that you don't remember with no idea of what took place. What a blessing, though, to have no recollection of it considering the cutting, tugging, ramming, as in the liposuction (I don't know if it was ramming, but that's what I envision), etc., that was going on. In my opinion, anesthesia and heavy pain medication are two of the greatest achievements in medicine. As inventions go, they rank right up there above Scotch Tape and sliced bread. I've watched surgeries like I had online and can't imagine going through such a thing with just a shot of whiskey and a bullet to bite on. Although back when that was the method, they weren't exactly performing breast augmentation.

The first couple of days were nothing but rest, pain meds, and ice packs. The usual at that point. My mom visited and fed us, my boys and husband were on call for my needs, but I spent most of the time with my animals. The dog never left my side, lying with me and protecting me from anyone who dared to come near. The cat visited in regular intervals and snuggled on her schedule. My dear friend, Nancy, came with lunch and brownies and good conversation. Those who are familiar with her brownies know how awesome that was. I reluctantly shared them with my family. Another dear friend, Pat, arrived with lunch and dinner, and treats. Friends and family are such a blessing! I don't recall many details of those first days due to the round-the-clock schedule of pain-eliminating Hydrocodone. The best thing happened 72 hours after surgery when I was able to shower. Without the drains needed in previous procedures, shower time came quicker, and it was wonderful. I keep mentioning the showers, but you take for granted the simple things until you have to forgo them for some time. Washcloth once overs and dry shampoo at the sink just aren't the same as standing there with that glorious water cascading down on you. I spent much longer in there than needed. My reach at that point wasn't great and everything hurt, so I didn't do much in the way of trying to scrub off the tape residue or wash off any of the orange surgical antiseptic or pen markings, I just stood and enjoyed the water.

Before I could shower, though, I had to unravel myself from all the gauze and tape that I was bound up in under the multitude of ace wraps. It was like unwrapping a surprise package. There was both anticipation and nervousness about what I was going to find inside. Have you ever gotten a grab bag? You pick it sight unseen and hope for the best. You want it to be a good surprise, but you know there's a chance that you'll be disappointed. It's not exactly the same as picking a $5 grab bag at a souvenir shop, something my boys did on our last vacation with less than exciting results, but you get the idea. I didn't actually expect anything negative but there was just a little twinge of wonder. It took nearly half an hour to remove all of the tape and bandaging. There has to be a better option than that medical tape, it's a real pain! Some areas that it was stuck to are completely numb and not an issue, but others were fairly tender, and I had to pull gently and slowly.

After removing a vanity top full of blood-soaked gauze and miles of sticky tape, all was revealed. I have learned in this journey that you need to be patient and that you can't take everything at immediate face value. The first time, I was told it would be about six months before everything was as it would be. I couldn't believe that would be true, but it was, almost to a tee. I know that it will take time for things to settle in and fall into place, for the swelling to completely go away and for the girls to show their true shape, but you can also tell fairly quickly if things look like they should. Amidst the bruising, oh my goodness the bruises, the steri-strips over the incisions, the tape residue, the pre-surgery drawings, and the leftover orange of the antiseptic, I could see that things looked favorable. I was pleased with what I saw. One of my biggest concerns was the state of my nipple tattoos, but no worries, they are great; placement is even better now. She did good!

After my first shower and a full glimpse at everything, I wrapped it all back up tightly. I would spend a bit more than another week like that, wrapping up daily after my shower as tight as bearable. Did I mention the bruising? I looked like I had been beaten. Did I take part in Fight Club while I was under? We'll never know because the first rule of Fight Club is you don't talk about Fight Club.

TIME KEEPS ON TICKING, TICKING, TICKING INTO THE FUTURE

July 12, 2017

Chemo Brain is real and doesn't go away when treatment ends. My memory is worse than ever, but I clearly remember June 3, and June 9, of 2014. On June 3, I was back at the mammography center going through tests and setting off on an unwanted journey. As I was dressing for work and putting on my American flag scarf this year on the day before the fourth, the same one that I wore then, I had a flash of standing in my manager's office telling her that it was likely a tumor, and I would keep her informed of what was to come. I said the words without realizing what they fully meant. Six days later, the confirmation call came and set everything in motion. It's funny how I can feel these days coming. This year I've reflected on my diagnosis anniversary in a bit of a depressive fog. I've been trying to ascertain for more than a week just what my problem is. I think it is a combination of adjusting to the current stage of my existence along with medication side effects and the chaos that disrupting and suppressing the sex hormones has on the female body and psyche. I'm not searching for sympathy, just laying it out honestly, as I have strived to do all along; wondering if this is normal at this point in the game. I'm struggling with this feeling of sadness mixed with uneasiness about what is or isn't happening in my life right now.

I believe I'm feeling the effects of a life interrupted. Three years ago, things were flowing along. I was adjusting to being a newlywed and we were building a life together. My boys were 14 and 18, and after years of working through the change in our family make up, we had hit a stride. My youngest was preparing to start high school and I was looking forward to what he would do with that and the experiences it would bring. Then I was struck head-on by the Big C. Newlywed bliss was halted, everything changed immediately. Focus shifted to preserving life. Physical changes combined with medication side effects, not to mention the mental stress of treatment, have worked against us in multiple ways. Not fair on either side. What if we had had those three years to bond and grow without the disruptions? Where would we be?

I was sidelined my son's entire freshman year and at various times in the years since. I feel like I wasn't fully there for him at a crucial time. I missed a lot. He was still a kid then, now he's a young man with a car, a job, a girlfriend, and a full social calendar. He'll be starting his senior year in just a few weeks. This phase of life is almost over. Time has been lost that can never be regained. My oldest son was at a different point when this all began, but I missed out on being fully present for him in times that he needed me, as well. Mom guilt is such a difficult thing to overcome.When this journey began, it was what it was, and I went with it. It was kind of like, "okay, this is where I am and this is what I'm doing with my life right now", and that's what I did. My life became a series of doctor visits and treatments and surgeries, and one thing dictated another, and I was present in it, and I was doing it and that's what was happening. I became the patient and the advocate and the fighter and the survivor. That was my focus and existence. Then, gradually, things slowed and dropped off and that is no longer what's happening. So now, where am I? I feel a bit lost.

I guess I'm supposed to return to life as usual and pick up where I left off, but I can't because it's not usual and won't ever be again. I am no longer a cancer patient and most of the treatment is over, but I will always carry some residuals with me from that time. I'm dealing with side effects of the post-cancer drug, my body is different, my memory is fuzzy, and my hair is super thin and still comes out by the handful. I'm lucky that it continues to grow and fill in as it falls out. Additionally, there is that little place in the back of my mind that is waiting for the other shoe to fall and hear the "C" word again. I'm sure I will always have that inkling back there no matter how hard I work to suppress it with percentages and likelihoods and examples. Any ache or pain or oddity stirs it up, and just for a moment, I feel a small twinge of panic. Par for the course of life on the other side, I suppose.

I'm in a transition period and I need to find my bearings. My life took an unexpected turn and veered onto a new path three years ago. After riding that out, now it has shifted again. I will straighten out the wheel and turn in the right direction, I just need to adjust my seat and get comfortable again. I am the driver in my life, and I know that it will head on the course that I set, but sometimes, you just need to pull over and stretch your legs.

August 7, 2017

It's my Three Year Cancerversary!

It was three years ago today that I had the mastectomy that the doctor says made me cancer-free. I'm that much closer to the all-important five-year mark. Thank you to Dr. W. for successfully removing the offending body parts, to Dr. B. for replacing them with ones that won't turn on me, and to Dr. G. for supporting me in my survivorship and to my awesome family and friends who have been there through it all! I literally couldn't have done it without you! HAPPY THREE TO ME!

June 19, 2018

Hey, there! How are you? Checking in with my pink and pink supporting friends. It's been a while since I've been on here. All is well, though, have just been out here living life. That's the point where things are currently and I'm not complaining at all. It's nice to be back to living on basic terms. There are still occasional reminders of what has transpired in the past few years, but they are not a focus most days. I can now power through a hot flash without missing a beat. I'm not saying that I don't sometimes freeze my family out with sub-zero air conditioning temps, and I may flip my fan off and on ten times a day at work, but I make those adjustments, wipe the sweat from my brow or from under my boobs or wherever and then move on.

July 3, 2018

July 3, 2014, the day that my life changed. This day, four years ago, is when everything began. It was the day of my first ever callback mammogram, which led directly to an ultrasound and then a biopsy. It will forever be the first of my pink anniversaries, one of three that pop up within about a month. This one will be followed shortly by my diagnosis day and then the date of my first surgery, the one that cleared the cancer. All of these dates are significant and all ones that bring about a feeling in my gut as they approach each year.

My terrible memory is legendary in my household. It's the details that get me. I can't spout off quotes from movies, like the rest of my family, or sometimes even remember that I saw the movie that they're talking to me about. I don't remember characters in books, I can't tell you what I was wearing when I had my first kiss or when my kids took their first steps, or even what I did on Wednesday of last week. Don't ask me the date of a famous event in history, and, if Facebook doesn't remind me of a birthday, or I don't write an appointment down on my work and home calendar, I'm probably going to forget it.

We used to have a large whiteboard on the kitchen door leading to our garage that I wrote everything on so it could be seen on the way out. My boys would tease that if it got wiped clean, I would have no idea what I was doing with my life. They were right and I lived in fear of that happening. It's a frustrating trait that I'm not a fan of and something that I know has worsened since chemo, but I've gotten used to it. At times I act as though I remember details just so I don't have to be embarrassed that I don't. That being said, certain things are embedded in my brain forever.

Some memories stay with me and elicit a deep feeling, for good or bad, when recalled. Good night kisses and toe pinches from a grandma with a face covered in Noxzema cold cream; being stretched out on the floor in front of a cozy fireplace watching Christmas classics with my cousins at my other grandma's house; my sixteenth birthday and the white Camaro with a big ribbon on it; the frightening wreck that totaled that beautiful car a month later; getting caught sneaking out and having to face my mom; my high school graduation; my wedding, both times; the births of my children; seeing my parents holding their first grandson; snuggling with and reading with my boys until they fell asleep; my mom's cancer diagnosis, both times; the phone call of a young family member's unexpected death; what I was doing on 9/11; the conversation when my children's father told me he was leaving; the evening that a wonderful man stunned me with a proposal and the day I saw my cancer on the ultrasound screen; these are some of the things that reside forever in my memory.

I see it as clear today as four years ago; that spot staring back at me from the screen and the sick feeling in the pit of my stomach when the ultrasound tech moved the wand under my arm. I knew she was looking at lymph nodes and I knew why. A few minutes later when the radiologist told me that it looked like a tumor, my tears were of acknowledgment, not of shock. I already knew it. And so it began, my new path, a new focus. A day that will forever stick with me and signifies a shift in direction. I try to look at it as an opportunity for personal growth and a tool to use my experiences to help others on the same path. That's how I reconcile the reason for it with myself, but it doesn't change the emotional weight of it, even as years pass.

As I'm writing this morning, I'm feeling sick to my stomach. I think I went too far in looking back; I usually try to look more forward. The emphasis needs to be on where I'm going, not where I've been; but you have to remember where you were and how you got here to appreciate where you are. That's either profound or complete nonsense, I'm not sure which or maybe a combination of the two. At any rate, this is the first of my upcoming "cancerversary" kind of days. I felt it coming, it has been a whisper in my ear the past few days. It's an odd feeling that I don't know if I can fully express, but anyone who has gone down the cancer path or a similar one of major illness can likely attest to. These are the things that mold us and make us who we are. I embrace it and acknowledge it and just wanted to share it.

July 9, 2018

Today is my pink D-day! Four years ago today, I was officially diagnosed with breast cancer. Stage 1, grade 3, triple positive. We didn't have that information right away, but that would end up being the result.

I am thankful for this day. That sounds odd. No one is thankful to be diagnosed with cancer, right? Of course not, I would have preferred not to have it, but since I did, I am thankful that it was diagnosed and found early so that it could be dealt with. I am thankful for the technology that identified the small spot, for the technicians that performed the tests to further investigate it, and the radiologists who read and interpreted those tests. I'm thankful for the wonderful medical facilities that I was treated in, for the compassionate nurses and reception staff who assisted me, and for the talented surgeons who met with me that day and set in motion, not only lifesaving but also self-image maintaining surgical treatment. I'm also thankful for my coworkers and employer who were supportive from the start. Most importantly, I'm thankful to God, who had His hand on me and my doctors from the beginning and to my tribe; my husband who had no idea what he was in for when he married me just nine months earlier, my two boys who bravely faced the fear of a mother's illness, my mom, who had faced the same disease twice herself and is the originating source of my strength, my dad, my in-laws, my extended family, two of my cousins in particular (you should both know who you are) and to my friends who all came together to lift me up and keep me going. I could look back on it as a terrible day, but I choose to look back on it with a thankful heart for the life that diagnosis preserved. Anniversary number two for year number four.

August 7, 2018

Today is my Celebration Day; four years cancer-free! It was four years ago this morning that I walked into the hospital with two boobs and a tumor and checked out the next day flat-chested and cancer-free. I didn't have a scan at the end of everything to declare me all clear, so today is the day that I choose to celebrate and count forward from. With all of the cancer being removed by surgery, nothing in my lymph nodes, and the chemo being preventative against possible microscopic disease, as my oncologist put it, this seems the logical date. A bone scan last fall showed no sign of tumors, so I believe all is still well.

Heading into the hospital that day in 2014, I had no idea just how many changes were ahead in my life and body, but each one has helped build strength. One more trip around the sun to reach that first huge cancer survivor milestone of 5 years. Almost there. That doesn't finalize anything, by any means, but it sure feels good to see it coming up fast. To those who have been on this ride with me, I say "Thank you and I Love You all!" To cancer, I say, "You had your chance and you failed. Good riddance to bad boobs!" I saw the best t-shirt today. It said, "Look out, I fight back!", with a pink ribbon hanging off the lettering. Enough said!!

October 10, 2018

According to Breastcancer.org, 330,080 women are expected to be diagnosed with breast cancer this year. Of those, 40,920 are expected to die from it, **BUT 289,160 will not!** It is not an instant death sentence.

Every scar tells a story.
Let yours speak loud enough to make a difference.

BREAST CANCER, IT'S NOT JUST FOR WOMEN ANYMORE

Raise your hand if you think breast cancer is only a woman's disease. If your hand is up, put it down, because that answer is wrong. And really, why would you put your hand up when you are sitting alone reading a book? Someone's going to walk in the room and see you sitting there with your hand in the air and start having serious doubts as to whether you should be left on your own. In all seriousness, despite breast cancer being primarily a woman's disease, it does not discriminate against the male species. If you have breasts, you can develop breast cancer.

Let me lay this out for you. The stats below come from internet sources that I trust to supply accurate and helpful information, *cancer.org,* which is the American Cancer Society's official page, and *breastcancer.org*. This same information can be found across many sites. For comparison purposes, I'm focusing on numbers for invasive breast cancer only. There are additional stats for cancer in situ, or non-invasive, and it can be broken down further, but it will only take a few general numbers to make my point.

Estimates for 2019 look like this:

- Expected new cases of diagnosed invasive breast cancer:

Women – more than 268,000

Men – around 2,670

- Lifetime risk of being diagnosed:

Women – about 1 in 8

Men – about 1 in 883

- Expected deaths due to invasive breast cancer:

Women – more than 41,000

Men – around 500

- Bottom line: Women are about 100 times more likely to be diagnosed with breast cancer, but some men will be diagnosed with and die from breast cancer this year, just the same as in years past.

Men tend to be mostly forgotten in discussions about breast cancer. That's understandable looking at the relatively small numbers to be diagnosed and die in relation to the female numbers; however, no number is too small if you or a loved one is among them. The statistics also don't reflect the number of men who may go undiagnosed, and subsequently die, due to a lack of knowledge or conversation about the disease, embarrassment of the situation, or failure to visit a doctor, as men will often do. As the mother of two sons who have an increased risk of this disease, I feel it is an important dialogue to have.

I never gave much thought to this subject until I encountered it. The month after mastectomy surgery, I attended my first *Pampered in Pink*. This is a free, social event put on by Making Strides Against Breast Cancer, a division of The American Cancer Society. Its purpose is to provide a few hours of pampering, fun, and support to breast cancer patients, survivors, and caregivers. In addition to the food, services, and giveaways, this gathering places you among a group of people who share a sense of what you are experiencing or have been through. Most are either also navigating it or have been there, done that. It was both encouraging and eye-opening for a newbie, like me.

Two important things happened that day as a result of the random table I chose to sit at; I encountered my first 30-year breast cancer survivor and had an important conversation with a male pink warrior.

It was a round table, so speaking to all seated there was easy. Being a bit of a social butterfly and still new to the pink life, I relished the opportunity to learn about my table mates. In talking to the lady on my left, I ascertained that she experienced breast cancer three decades prior and had been administered the dreaded "Red Devil". That treatment includes the chemo drug Doxorubicin (Adriamycin), which has a deep red color and is known to be especially toxic and bring on multiple, difficult side effects, hence its infamous name. She was a vibrant, attractive woman who appeared to be in her late 60s to early 70s. It was reassuring to know that this lady had fought and won in a time when there were fewer treatment options and much less known about the disease.

She not only overcame her cancer but had also survived the dangerous weapon used to battle it. A generation later, unfamiliar eyes could discern no outward signs of what she had been through. Meeting her gave me a stronger sense of hope for what was on my horizon. Meeting the lone male at the table, broadened my awareness.

Seated to my right was a couple, both dressed in pink shirts. My first thought was that the husband was supporting his wife by fully committing to the rosy color. What I soon came to know was that both members of the duo were breast cancer survivors. I was immediately curious about his experience and asked a few questions, which he happily obliged. They both appeared to be somewhere in their 60's and the wife had been first to take on cancer. It was because of her experience that he took seriously a potential issue of his own. He had come in from mowing the lawn one day with a troublesome pain in his breast. I honestly don't remember if he had felt a lump himself, but, regardless, he didn't hesitate to have it checked. The result was that the husband would become the recipient of a unilateral mastectomy, just like his wife. What a strong and unusual bond for a couple to have and what a great example they are and testament they have to share. I remember thinking how brave he was to be so open about his experience, an experience most men think could never happen to them. Four and a half years later, I would have an even deeper conversation with another courageous male survivor.

At some point, I came to know that my friend, Troy, had himself faced down breast cancer and persevered. It happened five years before I would travel the same path. His wife, Lori, and I had worked together in a health club office in the late 80s when I was but a mere pup. Being close in age and sharing the same sarcastic sense of humor and bubbly approach to life, Lori and I became fast friends. Fun times were had when hanging out with this lovely couple. As life and job changes will do, we lost touch until reuniting through social media years later. Having been acquainted with Troy for around 30 years or so, I could have never guessed that breast cancer would be something we would have in common. He graciously agreed to talk with me about his experience and share it with you here.

One night in August 2009, while sleepily exiting the bathroom, Troy veered too far to one side and ran into the door frame. As one will do to an area of bodily injury, he rubbed the sore spot on his chest to ease the pain. In doing so, he noticed an odd lump. In the light of day, he again inspected the area, finding the same protrusion and bringing it to the attention of his wife. He got in to see the doctor in September and was told that it was likely nothing serious as the mass was moveable and cancer is, typically, not. Fortunately, his doctor didn't rest on that likelihood but opted to test to be sure.

One thing that rings true in dealing with cancer is that every case is different and some deviate from the norm. It is also most often said that tumors don't hurt. Many take that to mean that a breast lump that hurts couldn't be cancerous, which is a dangerous belief to hold. I have talked to several survivors and read many accounts that begin with a painful lump that turned out to be cancer. Never fail to investigate something questionable based on "most of the time" outcomes. It's your health, question everything and pursue it until you have an answer that you are satisfied with.

The first week of October found Troy doing something he never imagined himself to do, he went in for a mammogram. He was given a pink gown to wear, there were no other color options, and was escorted to his own room away from the women waiting to be tested. He expressed that he didn't mind being in the same area as the women but found that his segregation was not to save him embarrassment but to ensure the comfort of the ladies. He also got to experience the fun of the nipple BB bandage, like the ones I talked about earlier. When it was his turn, he was taken in for a mammogram. They have a way of getting any type of mammary into the pancake-making machine, so him being a man wasn't an issue for the tech. Troy's take on the mammogram experience is simply, "It hurt!!"

After the mammogram, he went for a biopsy. He was told they would take six samples but stopped after four. The radiologist said that was enough. That was worrisome to him. When you are in that spot, you analyze everything looking for signs. You're searching for anything to tell you that it's all okay, but you keep coming up with things that point to your worst thought. As with myself and any other who's been in that situation, his wait for the biopsy results was torturous. As Friday was ending, he could wait no longer and so contacted the doctor's office. The nurse said that she couldn't give him the results, the doctor wanted to see him the next week. Troy persisted and insisted that he get an answer. He and Lori's sanity would not survive the weekend with that question hanging in the air. As Troy so aptly put it, they don't call you into the doctor's office to give you good news. The nurse finally relented, and he was told that he did in fact have breast cancer.

When the details came out, Troy would know that he had a

2.2cm tumor, stage 2A invasive ductal carcinoma that was hormone receptive. After surgery, he would find out that there was no lymph node involvement. His cancer was very similar to what I would face years later but with a couple of discrepancies; mine was one stage less and his was HER2-negative, making it less aggressive in the grading. My stage was earlier, but grade was more aggressive, he was at the next stage, but the grading was less aggressive. A fine example of how cancer can be similar, but at the same time, very different. I also found it interesting that his male breast cancer was estrogen positive. Apparently, most male breast cancer is hormone receptive. We forget that men have estrogen, just like women have testosterone. As men age, their testosterone levels decrease, and estrogen levels increase. For this reason, most men who develop breast cancer are older. Troy was on the younger side for his diagnosis and would have been under the radar for the disease. It turned out to be a blessing that he ran into that doorway and found the lump when he did. Had it gone unnoticed for longer, his experience could have been a much more dire one.

The cancer diagnosis came on Friday and by the next Tuesday, the couple was in the doctor's office creating a treatment plan. He would have a unilateral mastectomy without reconstruction followed by 16 rounds of chemo, then five years of Tamoxifen. The doctor said he could get Troy in for surgery on the coming Friday. The quick surgery time gave Lori a flash of panic. She figured that it must be extremely bad for the surgeon to rush him in so fast. When the doctor realized how it was looking to them, he confirmed that they just lucked out and a surgery slot was open due to a cancellation, not that it was so urgent that they had to get it out rapidly. Troy was fine with that quick arrangement. He expressed feeling the same thing that I did when I got my diagnosis, he wanted it out, right then. In that instance, you know that it doesn't belong there, and you just want it out as soon as possible. Troy would leave the office that day armed with a package of informational pamphlets slipped nicely into a little pink bag.

With only three days between the doctor visit and scheduled surgery, there wasn't much time to process what was happening and there was a lot to take in. The couple went home and dove headfirst into the information they had been given. One pamphlet explained what happens during a mastectomy, recovery, etc. Another talked about chemo and explained the possible side effects. Troy quickly discovered that the information that he had was geared toward females. Nothing in any of the materials talked about how breast cancer affects men. As they were both learning what was to come, Troy couldn't help but let his wife in on one of the concerning side effect possibilities that he may face during chemo.

"Oh no, Lori, this might be bad!"

"What?!? What is it?", said his terrified wife.

"Well," Troy said, "this says that I may experience vaginal discharge."

Absorb that for a moment. I can only hope that as he sat there laughing heartily, Lori winged one of the pamphlets right at him and then found it in herself to laugh, too. They both chuckle about it now. You have to find the humor and I would say that he sure found it there. An important lesson from that interaction is that there needs to be breast cancer information available that includes how it affects men and what they may experience during treatment. Providing a man with information telling him that he may experience vaginal issues is as helpful as telling a woman that she may have pain in her testicles.

Troy had a successful mastectomy to remove his cancerous breast. He completed his 16 rounds of chemo over five months, the first four treatments taking place every two weeks with the remaining 12 happening weekly. He lost his hair, had some taste changes, and was tired after treatment, but continued to work and attempted to maintain as much normalcy as possible. Although he didn't experience any lady part excretions during chemo, he was gifted with gallstones, a pulmonary embolism, and a blood clot in his leg. He also completed a five-year course of daily Tamoxifen. It was five years after completing all of that when I spoke with him. At the time of this writing, he remains cancer-free and retains his humor about the experience.

Talking with Troy made me realize that there should be more done for our men regarding this disease. We need to have open conversations and remove the stigma of male breast cancer. Men should be encouraged to check their breasts and see a doctor regarding any abnormalities without feeling embarrassed.

AND THE BEAT GOES ON

August 7, 2019

This is the day that I have waited for since August 7, 2014. It has been five years since my complete, double mastectomy surgery. TODAY I AM 5 YEARS CANCER-FREE!!

In the life of a survivor, this is a big day! Reaching the five-year benchmark without any recurrence or occurrence of new cancer brings the expectation that it is less likely for a return of the original disease. Of course, there are no guarantees and I know better than to let my guard down. A survivor is always waiting for the other shoe to drop. I will expect that shoe to stay put but keep my eyes open.

I didn't reach this point alone. I have a wonderful support system and the best doctors, nurses, and medical care. Thank you to all of you who are in my life! My husband and sons, my parents and in-laws, my family, especially my cousins, wonderful friends, my co-workers, neighbors, Dr. W., Dr. B., Dr. G., my general practitioner, and each of their nurses and staff have all played a part in getting me here. I appreciate and love you all! And, as always, to God be the glory!

That post wrapped up the first five years of my life as a breast cancer survivor. It solidified me as a number in the total of those alive five years after diagnosis. Currently in September 2021, I'm into year seven and hope to reach the upper limits of the survivor stats.

Putting this together was often emotional. Some aspects were difficult to relive while others brought back feelings and memories that I appreciated. My intention was to share it all; the good, the bad, the painful, the unexpected and even the humor. While the process was cathartic for me, my hope is that this will help others navigating the pink nightmare to know that they aren't alone in their feelings and experiences, to find hope, tips and even a different way to look at things. Additionally, I wanted to give perspective to those on the outside; to show the ups and downs of a cancer diagnosis and treatment in order to better understand the reality of the person going through it.

I always hated the "I feel sorry for you" look that I would get at times. That, when paired with the slightly head-cocked, soft-voiced question of, "How *are* you?", would bring to the surface a sense of defiance. It wasn't the question itself, but rather the way it was asked. Instead of a scarlet letter A on my chest, I sometimes felt like I had a giant C stamped on my forehead that elicited pity and sadness from others. I didn't want that. I appreciated the kindness, compassion and understanding that I received, but I didn't want people to feel sorry for me in a "she's doomed" sort of way. I knew what I was facing and what I had to go through to find victory, but I believed in my personal resolve to prevail and needed others to show that they did, too.

I realize that most people don't exude that on purpose, it's just how it comes out. I get it! I know that I have likely given someone else that look. I'm the person who can hold things in and not say what my inner self is screaming, but my face will often betray me. There is a t-shirt that I'm going to get one of these days that says, "Did I roll my eyes out loud?" That is me in a nutshell. I am more careful now and would ask others to think about it, too. Don't fail to show that you care or ask about the circumstance but do it with confidence in the person you are talking to. Obviously, don't blow smoke, read the room and the situation. Most will appreciate compassion rather than pity.

So much has taken place in these past seven years; every happening an opportunity for learning and growth. I went from a second-time newlywed with a fresh cancer diagnosis to a single again survivor on the other side of 50. I now see myself differently and look at life through a clear lens. I'm convinced I can handle whatever it has to offer. I may need time to adjust and get my bearings, but then there is no stopping me. I am fully comfortable in my new skin. This journey has taught me to better appreciate my life and the people in it and to strive to be more patient and thoughtful of those around me. My faith has also been strengthened through my trials. I know more than ever that God mans the controls in my life, I have seen it time and again. He's got this!

I realize that many have a much harder time than I did, and I don't take that for granted. No cancer experience is easy, but some are much worse than others and survival isn't always an option. I wish that were never the case and I would not insinuate that all can be boiled down to something you can overcome and move on from. I can only pull from my experiences and take the lessons that they afforded.

I hope that you have enjoyed this book and I thank you for allowing me to share my thoughts and experiences with you. I appreciate you taking time out of your life to look into mine. With that I say, check your boobs, be aware of your health, applaud the people you hold dear and never underestimate yourself. Smell the roses and eat the chocolate because you deserve the things that make life sweet.

- Lisa

Appreciation

I have given thanks in these pages over and over again to the point that you're likely tired of reading it, but it's time to call out some people by name.

Rebecca Knoles – my mom
Thank you for everything! Details in the dedication.
Jacob Stratton – my firstborn
Thank you for the hours you sat with, entertained, and supported me in all stages of my treatment and recovery.
Sam Stratton – my baby boy
Thank you for proudly and publicly supporting me by wearing pink during my chemo and for being there always.
Johnie Knoles – my dad
Thank you for always being in my corner and encouraging me. I know you would have been proud of this. I'm sorry you weren't still here to see it.
Eric Woods – once my husband, always my friend
Thank you for being with me in every step of my journey; for all that you did then and for helping me put this together.
Greg and Lynn Woods – my awesome in-laws
Thank you for your love, help and support.
Dr. Keith Wichterman, MD – my surgeon
Thank you for removing the cancer and guiding me forward.
Dr. Beth Bergman, MD – my plastic surgeon
Thank you for reconstructing my chest and for your smiles.
Dr. Amit Gupta, MD – my oncologist
Thank you for watching after me and fielding my questions.
Paul Bessette – my tattooist
Thank you for the amazing artwork that you blessed me with.
Heather Cheek – my cousin and nip trip partner
Thank you for always jumping in and being there for me.
Kim Hurley – my cousin and partner in crime
Thank you for your total support that continues without fail.
Jami Stephens – first my friend, now my cousin
Thank you for being there then and supporting me still.

Stephanie Warren – my supportive cousin
Thank you for being a voice in my corner.
Andrea Larsson – my friend since second grade
Thank you for the phone calls and being there all these years.
Georgine Stephens – my wonderful aunt
Thank you for wrapping up my chemo and cheering me on.
Nancy Galligan – my lovely friend
Thank you for always being there with love and compassion.
Sonya Dilley – my artist friend and cheerleader
Thank you for the perfectly amazing painting that became
this cover and for your constant encouragement and support.
Troy and Lori Wetter – my friends from long ago
Thank you for allowing me to share your story.
Kellby Gietl – my co-worker and friend
Thank you for opening up to me and exposing your story.
Pat Kuster – my friend and bald stylist
Thank you for shaving my head and for all your support.

And to:
My Stephens family – all of you crazy people
My gang of friends – each and every one
My chemo nurses
My Springfield Clinic nurses
My Memorial Medical Center nurses and techs
The receptionists and all staff at those centers
Anyone else who has shown me kindness in this
There are far too many of you to call each out by name, but I
appreciate every person who has shown me love and support,
aided in my medical care, brought my family food, sent a
card, made a visit, provided a service, sat with me, talked
with me, prayed for me, or simply gave me a smile and a kind
word. I am a woman truly blessed; my treasures are not
measured in gold.

**And finally, to the reader who doesn't fit into any of
the categories above:**
I appreciate you taking your time and giving me a voice.

Made in the USA
Monee, IL
25 August 2023

41643253R00195